MONEY DOESN'T GROW ON TREES

MONEY DOESN'T GROW ON TREES

The Friendliest Guide to Personal Finance

Lavanya Mohan

SIMON & SCHUSTER

London · New York · Sydney · Toronto · New Delhi

Published in India by Simon & Schuster India, 2025

Copyright © Lavanya Mohan, 2025

The right of Lavanya Mohan to be identified as author of this work has been asserted by her in accordance with Section 57 of the Copyright Act 1957.

1 3 5 7 9 10 8 6 4 2

Simon & Schuster India
818, Indraprakash Building,
21, Barakhamba Road,
New Delhi 110001.

www.simonandschuster.co.in

Paperback ISBN: 978-81-983564-3-7
eBook ISBN: 978-81-983564-2-0

Typeset in India by SŪRYA, New Delhi
Printed and bound in India by Replika Press Pvt. Ltd.

Simon & Schuster India is committed to sourcing paper that is made from wood grown in sustainable forests and support the Forest Stewardship Council, the leading international forest certification organisation. Our books displaying the FSC logo are printed on FSC certified paper.

No part of this publication may be reproduced, transmitted or stored in a retrieval system, in any form or by any means, electronic, mechanical, photocopying, recording or otherwise, without the prior permission of the publisher.

The views and opinions expressed in this book are the author's own and the facts are as reported by her and which have been verified to the extent possible, and the publishers are not in any way liable for the same. The author has made all reasonable effort to contact copyright-holders for permissions. In case there are omissions or errors in the form of credits given, corrections may be made in future editions.

This book is sold subject to the condition that it shall not, by way of trade or otherwise, be lent, resold, hired out, or otherwise circulated, without the publisher's prior consent, in any form of binding or cover other than that in which it is published.

CONTENTS

Preface

I spent 3 months as a new apprentice in a chartered accountant's office, doing tax audits of individuals—people like you and me. I'd come to office, I'd be handed fat files that contained the financial histories of these individuals, and I'd have to scour through these statements, line after line, day after day. I still remember my co-apprentices, clucking their tongues sympathetically each time they saw me being handed a new file to audit. You see, they were learning to audit companies and corporations—they had accounting and auditing standards to adhere to, complex balance sheets to be made, and audit reports to be written, while I went through grocery receipts. That put them on top of the apprenticeship food chain and me at the bottom.

Not that I cared. I imagined myself to be a surgeon who, calmly but minutely, examined the innards of these unknown people who laid naked on my cold table. It wasn't long before I started noticing patterns. There were loud differences in the spending habits between people who were middle-aged and people who were younger. The majority of my older clients were conservative in the way they spent their money. They invested regularly in some plan or the other, rarely swiped their credit cards, and seemed content with spending money on just the essentials, with shopping restricted to festive periods.

Younger clients, on the other hand, seemed more carefree. They spent frequently, swiped their credit cards with enthusiasm, and had dangerously low balances at the end of each month. These balances would then be replenished either by parent or by pay check, after which the cycle would start all over again.

These observations, while amusing at that point, started hitting differently as time passed.

Sometime around May 2016, *BuzzFeed*, the internet news giant, published an article by the freelance journalist Gayatri Jayaraman titled, 'The Urban Poor You Haven't Noticed: Millennials Who're Broke, Hungry, But On Trend'[1]. The essay, which explored how young, well-educated Indians were living out of their means to project an appearance of being well-heeled, only to find themselves starving, evicted, and living out of their cars, went viral within the hour of its publication. The essay's title may have been poorly worded, but it did spark conversation about the toxic cocktail of easy credit, poor fiscal habits, and the pressure to have an enviable Instagram lifestyle that drugged an entire generation from saving efficiently.

And then came the pandemic.

Between the haze of March 2020 and March 2022, India's financial landscape became a financial…amusement park. The heady combination of boredom, spare cash, and sparse knowledge encouraged millions of middle-class Indians to become stock-market investors. Between March

2020 and March 2024, the number of demat accounts in India grew fourfold—from 40 million, to 150 million. This unprecedented gusto of the Indian retail investor was one of the better twists that the pandemic served us.

We also saw:

- ⇨ Cryptocurrency waves that went bust before you could say boom.
- ⇨ Twenty-something 'finfluencers' gaining more legitimacy over finance professionals who'd been in the business for twenty-something years.
- ⇨ Buy-now-pay-later schemes making shopaholics out of savers.
- ⇨ Hospital bills driving families into debt.
- ⇨ Young India is staring at a 5-year low in household savings. The Ministry of Statistics and Programme Implementation (MOSPI) has released data that savings has been on a downtrend since 2020–21 and that household savings have fallen by over ₹9 lakh crore between 2020–21 and 2022–23[2].

It's not looking good.

And it makes you wonder: Why is it that millennials, this generation that is so adept at managing multiple hobbies and social networks, that is otherwise so woke, so terrible at managing money?

I believe it is a combination of two things at play. The first is our education system—it has failed us. It doesn't matter which board in India you may have studied in, you just don't learn about money or taxes or anything resembling money management in school or in college.

me: what are taxes and how do I pay them?
school system: worry not
school system: mitochondria is the powerhouse of the cell

Source: invisiblehallows

722,283 notes  

The second reason is that while Indians enjoy talking about money, discussions are often restricted to gossip about the wealth of others and the rising price of tomatoes. Indian parents are guarded about their own savings and almost never discuss their retirement plans with their children.

Worse still, most don't save for retirement in the belief that their children will take care of them when they age. On the flip side, although Indian children are constantly *told* to save, they aren't *taught* how to. And if you're a woman in India, you're actively encouraged to stay away from money management beyond grocery budgets.

It's of little surprise then, that we end up navigating finance with unreliable sources—social media, the murky corners of Reddit, and through arbitrary conversations with our peers. And while experts are now more accessible than ever, they are not approachable. Their language continues to be technical, intimidating, and borderline condescending.

I guess what I'm trying to say is: We deserve better. And that's why this book exists.

Through the course of the next several chapters, I'll share stories, numbers, the occasional meme, and everything else I know about money. We'll talk about budgets, bank accounts, tax, investing, and Instagram lifestyles.

If you've ever been stressed or intimidated by personal finance, worry not, the answers are here. By the end of this book, you'll not only know how money works, but also how to manage your money and make it grow.

You've got this!

Notes

1. Gayathri Jayaraman, 'The Urban Poor You Haven't Noticed: Millennials Who're Broke, Hungry, But On Trend', *BuzzFeed*, 5 May 2016. https://www.buzzfeed.com/gayatrijayaraman/broke-hungry-and-on-trend
2. TNN, 'Net FY 23 Household Savings Hits 5 Year Low', *The Times of India*, 8 May 2024. https://timesofindia.indiatimes.com/business/india-business/net-fy23-household-savings-hit-5-year-low/articleshow/109930489.cms

1

Our Relationship with Money

What Does Money Say about You?

Your financial status has nothing to do with who you are as a person. And yet, who you are as a person will have a significant impact on your financial status.

Our relationship with money is deeply entrenched with our own personalities. The way we handle money is often a reflection of ourselves—our gender, our upbringing, our childhood, our aspirations, and our trauma. It's so deep that even the words we use to describe other people often have money laced connotations. Generous, miserly, shrewd, careless.

And that's why we get so affected when people talk to us about money. We don't look at it as a conversation about our finances. We look at it as a conversation about us. If we're asked to save a little more, we don't see it as financial advice. We see it as an accusation and interpret it as callousness. We get defensive. If we're asked to spend differently, or make different buying choices, we go to great lengths to justify our expenses because we see it as a direct attack on our tastes. And God forbid someone questions our investments—that just shows that they think we're dumb.

But this isn't just about them. The flipside is that we also get very judgemental in matters of money. When someone in our circle buys something expensive, for example, we rarely judge the *transaction*. We judge *them*. It's not unusual for us to say, 'Oh this is nice, but *I could never* spend so much on a phone/dress/trip.' Judgement isn't reserved for just the big spenders either. 'I could never sacrifice my comfort to save a few thousand,' we tell those on a budget.

It's as if the very mention of money gives one permission to open the floodgates of judgement. And naturally, it's because of how often and how strongly we judge those around us, that we automatically hesitate talking about our own finances. It's one thing for us to call someone kanjoos. But *them* calling *you* kanjoos? Forget about it. Worse still, what if they think your investing choices are stupid? That *you're stupid?*

The way we judge others' finances is the best reflection of how we feel about our own finances. It's probably the best indicator of our relationship with money.

And the truth is that one does not have to detach to understand their relationship with money. Just observation is a good starting point. Why do you save the way you do? Why do you spend the way you do? What do you think happened in your life to make you look at money the way you do? Acknowledging your relationship with money and being honest with yourself about your finances is the first step towards financial independence.

Think of it as a map. The map has every road, alleyway, and landmark plotted on it. But you're not going to all of them—and only you know which destination truly matters. When you take a hard look at your money habits—whether it's your spending, saving, or even your thoughts around financial security—you'll be able to pinpoint where exactly you're starting from on the map.

And from there, you can decide where you want to head. A dream financial milestone (maybe a house), a future free of financial stress, living a debt-free life, or maybe you want to take the scenic route which incorporates all of these milestones one after the other.

But remember, you need to be very sure about where you are starting in order to get to where you're supposed to be. If you're not honest about your financial present, or don't have a clear set of destinations in mind, even the best, most detailed maps can have you lost and wandering aimlessly.

Do You Speak Money?

Money is a lot like high school mathematics, in that, perfectly intelligent people who are fully capable of mastering the subject are convinced that they will just not get it.

I don't think I'll ever understand it, they'll say, and give up before they begin. Well, as someone who enjoys both subjects, let me assure you, money is not at all like mathematics. In fact, it's like French. And much like French—or art appreciation, nutrition, fitness, Korean pop culture, and the Marvel Universe for that matter—money is just a language, with its own vocabulary, grammar, and rules.

If reading financial news has always made you feel like it's something you won't understand, it's because it's another language. The good news is that the language of money is very easy to learn.

Grammar

Let's start at the very beginning. The alphabets of money are the very fundamental ways in which money behaves and sometimes, misbehaves. We're constantly told to save, to invest, to have insurance, and to think long-term. But we're rarely told *why* we must do it, which is why we don't feel compelled to. When you learn the mechanics, the rules, and the grammar with which money operates, on the other hand, you'll have greater conviction to take charge of your finances and a much stronger grip on the subject.

Time Value of Money

If you've ever lived with talkative grandparents, you've already been exposed to Time Value of Money, which is nothing but the technical term for your grandparents whining about how they used to buy gold for ₹10 back in the day. Time Value of Money is the idea that money today is worth more than money tomorrow.

It's vital that we talk about Time Value of Money before we even think about saving or investing because understanding this concept is vital for making sound financial decisions—not just in the long term, but every single day.

Let's say someone asks you to choose between taking ₹1 lakh today and ₹1 lakh in a year's time. Which option should you choose? You should choose to take the first option, because that ₹1 lakh today is capable of earning interest and transforming to a sum of money that's more than a lakh. So, the sooner you receive your money, the greater its value.

I'm going to take a minute to stress on the word 'value' here, because when it comes to money, value is dynamic. What ₹1 lakh can get you today is not the same as what ₹1 lakh can get you 10 years from now. ₹1 lakh in the mid-80s meant a nice apartment in the middle of the city. ₹1 lakh today is only capable of getting you furniture. The amount of money—₹1 lakh—hasn't changed, but its value has. Twenty years from now, the value of ₹1 lakh is only going to deteriorate further.

And that's why the Time Value of Money is an essential concept to know—to the point where it's the first lesson you learn when you study finance. We must use the concept of Time Value of Money to estimate future needs, especially in the far future. You might think you only need a certain amount of money to live your life a certain way, but chances are that you will be needing much more to live your life that way.

So, there are two takeaways here:

- ⇨ The first is that money, when invested, grows over time
- ⇨ The second is that when money is left idle, it loses value over time

Inflation

Inflation refers to the increase in the prices of goods and services over time. Inflation and Time Value of Money are essentially two sides of the same coin. It refers to reduced purchasing power, which is a technical way of saying that the same ₹10 which could get you gold in the 50s, can only get you a half cup of tea today.

So, what causes inflation? There are 3 broad reasons:

1. Demand-Pull: Prices rise when the demand for something is far greater than the supply or availability of it. Let's say your favourite café suddenly goes viral on Instagram. Before you know it, every seat is occupied and reservation backlogs go into weeks. This lack of availability will push people into paying higher prices for the same product, leading to price rise. The café owner will see the rush and jack his prices up. And just like that, your morning pick-me-up becomes more expensive, not because the cost of ingredients has increased, but because the number of people willing to pay for it (aka demand) has increased. Late night or peak time Uber/cab prices are another example. This is called Demand-Pull inflation.

2. Currency in Circulation: When a country prints money excessively, there is more currency in circulation than usual. Too much cash in circulation reduces the value of money because more money chases the same things. And when there's more money to chase the same thing, demand goes up. And when demand goes up, so do prices.

3. **Cost-Pull:** Prices rise when there are issues with supply, even if demand remains the same. This is particularly relevant during times of crisis, both natural (think floods), and man-made (lockdowns). When supply is cut off, prices soar. This is called Cost-Pull inflation.

These are the basic mechanics of inflation. The inflation that happens in our country is usually a result of a combination of the factors explained above.

Why Should You Care about Inflation?

You should care because inflation will eat into your savings. Remember that our life expectancy rates are higher than they've ever been before, as are old-age-related medical complications. Yes, ₹5 lakh might be enough for an emergency hospitalisation today, *but will it be enough in*

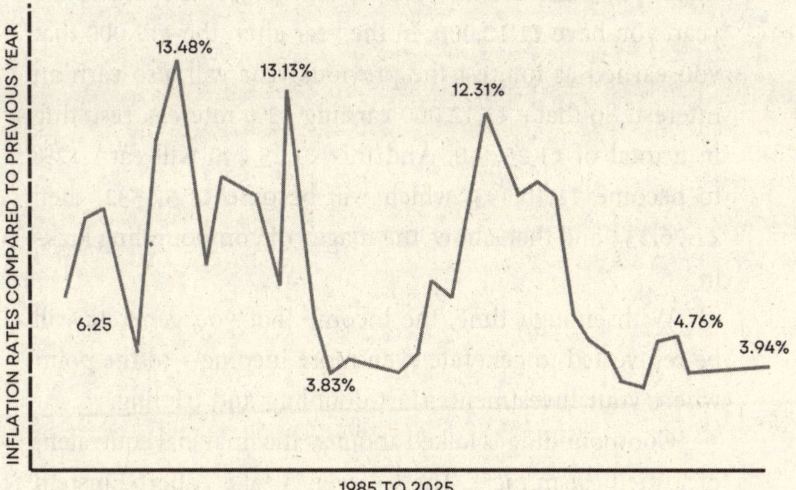

5 years' time? ₹40 lakh might be enough for a higher education degree today, but will it be enough in 10 years' time? It is vital to think about your savings with respect to inflation and see if you're saving enough to cover for your future goals.

This chart on the opposite page represents inflation rates in India year on year from 1985. Do not be misled by the dips. They do not mean that prices decreased. They just indicate that price rise happened, but at a lower rate.

Compounding

Compounding is when the income or interest that you receive on your investment is reinvested to earn more income. Think of it as incomeception—where your income earns income earns income earns...you get the picture.

Let's say you have ₹1,00,000. You put it in a deposit that'll pay you 12% interest per annum. At the end of the year, you have ₹1,12,000. In the year after, the ₹12,000 that you earned as interest the previous year will also earn an interest. So that's ₹1,12,000 earning 12% interest, resulting in a total of ₹1,25,440. And this ₹1,25,440 will earn 12% to become ₹1,40,493, which will become ₹1,57,532, then ₹1,76,234 and that's how 'the magic' of compounding kicks in.

With enough time, the income that you generate will be reinvested to generate even more income—to the point where your investments start doubling and tripling.

Compounding is talked about as the financial equivalent of a medical miracle. There's even a fake Albert Einstein quote about how it's the '8th wonder of the world'. But in order for compounding to work this level of sorcery with our money, we need to talk about the 3 very important factors:

1. Time: Compounding's 'magic' will not kick in if you don't give it time. And by time, I don't mean a few years, we're talking about a few decades. Morgan Housel writes in his (fantastic) book, *The Psychology of Money*, about how the bulk of Warren Buffet's wealth actually came into place when he was in his 60s, 50 whole years after he started investing. Compounding cannot be successful without time.

2. Consistent Investing: Compounding isn't effective when you invest once and forget about it. You need to be able to invest consistently and continuously over a period of time to reap its benefits.

Take the previous example. ₹1,00,000 invested once and compounded for 20 years at 12% is roughly ₹9 lakh. But if you invest ₹1,00,000 *year after year* for 20 years at 12%, you'll have approximately ₹81 lakh at the end of 20 years. That's a lot of money. And if you want that money, you've got to be consistent with your investments.

3. The Rate of Return: The trickiest part of compounding is finding investments that offer returns which are capable of beating inflation. 12% per annum compounded annually sounds amazing, except very few investments offer that rate of growth (for reference, FDs compound at the rate of approximately 5% per annum).

In order to have your money compound at double digit rates, or at the very least, rates which are capable of beating inflation, you need to have a basket or a portfolio of diverse investments with varying rates of return to achieve your goals.

Liquidity

Liquidity refers to an investment's ability to convert into cold, hard cash. Therefore, it refers to your ability to generate cash at short notice with ease and at a fair value for your investment. If you were to visualise liquidity as a pyramid, then bank accounts and cash would be right on top, as the most liquid.

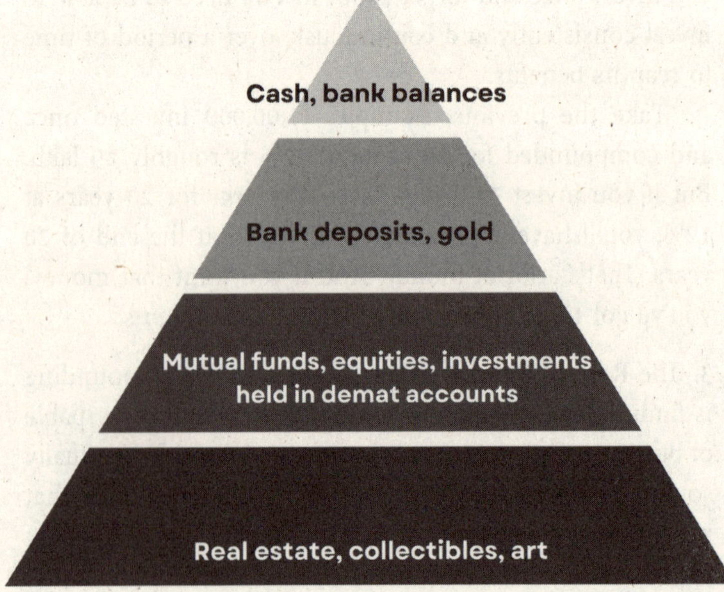

This would be followed by bank deposits, which are easy to access although there is a penalty for withdrawal before it matures. After this comes gold, with digital taking precedence before physical.

Mutual funds and equity investments come next, because while they are simple enough to convert into cash or liquidate, you are paying the price of future growth. So, your liquidation might not be at a fair value.

Bonds are trickier to liquidate, because they're usually locked in for a certain period of time.

Real estate sits at the bottom, given the time, effort, and paperwork they need to be converted into cash.

And finally, the least liquid of investments are the ones whose value is entirely subjective, like art, or investments that might not have an active market of buyers, like a stamp or coin collection.

The Four Pillars of Money

Time Value of Money, Inflation, Compounding and Liquidity are the four concepts that you need to drill into your head before you embark on any journey with money.

If you've only vaguely caught the concepts, I beseech you to take the time to understand them. Maybe you can read the chapter again (because what are re-reads between friends?) until it's solidified. I say this because you can't ride the chariot of financial freedom without having control over these four (slightly wild) horses that are tethered to it. The good news is that once you do, you'll realise that they all come together to say the same thing: Save well and save better, because if you don't, you're screwed.

Women and Money

Sometime in 2016, when I was working as a Chartered Accountant in Practice in Chennai, a client requested me to conduct an 'educational' session on the basics of finance for a group of women. I agreed, expecting to talk to women from similar backgrounds who were just getting started with organising their finances.

That, however, was not the case. I ended up talking to women whose names and signatures commanded conglomerates and carried a great heft of money, power, and influence. Some of their handbags were—and continue to be—worth more than my annual income. But all of them, it seemed, shared a common insecurity for numbers.

Finance, financial statements, and all associated terminology overwhelmed them. It didn't help that whenever they sat in meetings, they held themselves back from asking for clarifications about their own company out of fear of being pushed over or being subjected to condescension from senior male members in the room who employed financial jargon with ease.

That women in power go through the same motions that the rest of us do was very telling for me. If women in the uppermost echelons of society were having issues comprehending money, then what about the rest of us? Historically, women have always been left behind when it comes to matters of money. While plenty of women do have and operate their own bank accounts, they are rarely included in conversations about financial planning.

A survey run by a Life Insurance Company[1] on financial

awareness among women revealed that 59% do not independently take decisions on their finances. The survey also stated that 89% of married women depend on their spouses for financial planning. This isn't to say that marriage is a deterrent to a woman's financial independence, but that men make the crucial financial decisions of the household by default. If it's not the husband making investments or buying insurance, it's the father or the brother. Insurance, mutual funds, long-term savings aren't discussions that we have.

The financial discussions that we do have, are relegated to managing the grocery budget (the survey even said that for 39% of its respondents, financial planning was restricted to just this).

Additionally, a great percentage of women continue to be reliant on their spouses/parents for money (it's been established that India ranks very poorly in terms of women's participation in the workforce). And even working women—as high as 59% in urban India and 65% in Tier 3 cities—don't take financial decisions independently. All of this snowballs into not only widespread financial illiteracy among women, but also ensures that it is difficult for women to become truly financially independent.

But perhaps the most significant struggle when it comes to women taking charge of their finances are the social consequences of our failure. Gender has nothing to do with investment decision-making. Men make financial mistakes all the time. But when they fail, the social consequences that they face are rarely as damning as the ones that women face when they fail. We're constantly told to stay in our lanes, take care of our homes, and leave the 'money business' to the men—even if they don't know any better.

It is empowering to know how money works—irrespective of your gender—but it is especially important for women to have this knowledge. We save differently, spend differently, and have very different financial goals. We live longer but end up with more—and sometimes permanent—breaks in our career. We run out of money much quicker than we expect to. And we fool ourselves into thinking that we won't 'get' money.

Well, it's time to go get it.

Our Relationship with Money—The TL; DR

Here's what I want you to take away from this chapter:

Your *Money Habits Are NOT Like* Their *Money Habits*

The way you spend, save, or stress about money is a reflection of who you are—your childhood, your goals, and yes, even your baggage. There's no one size fits all approach, and everyone's financial histories are as unique and complicated as their family histories. Don't beat yourself up for it. Just being aware of your habits is enough to chart a path forward.

Money Is Not *Math. It's a Language*

Finance jargon is the same kind of gibberish that French and Chinese is. It's a language that needs to be learned. If you can decode nutrition labels, skincare ingredients, or speak a third language, you're well on track to speaking finance. Once you get the hang of the basic 'grammar', it's way less intimidating.

Cash Doesn't Look Good in the Future

A rupee today is worth more than a rupee tomorrow because it can grow. That's why holding onto cash without investing is like leaving fruit out—it'll go bad.

Inflation Can Eat You

Inflation is the reason why your grandmother could buy a month's groceries for ₹10 back in the day, but today, that amount won't even get you chai. If your savings—and income—aren't keeping up with inflation, you're basically losing money.

The Magic of Compounding

Money makes money. The good news is that you don't need to be a billionaire to see this in action. With compounding, the income you earn on your investments will start earning its own income, PROVIDED you give it time and show up consistently (like a good fitness routine).

Liquidity = How Fast You Can Get That Cash

Liquidity is just a straight-cut way of saying how quickly you can turn something into actual money. Your savings account? Super liquid. Your flat? Not so much.

The Fantastic Four of Finance

Time value of money, inflation, compounding, and liquidity. If you get these four, your personal finance game is already next level.

Girls Just Wanna Have Funds

Even super accomplished women often let someone else handle the money stuff—it's a mix of societal conditioning and lack of confidence. But money has nothing to do with gender. So, it's time to get into the driver's seat.

Financial Illiteracy Is Expensive

Relying on friends, influencers, or sketchy Reddit threads for money advice can backfire. Learning the basics means fewer 'what did I just sign up for?' moments.

Money Isn't a Dirty Word

The more you talk about it, the more normal it becomes. It's only when you understand your finances that you gain the greatest flex of our current era—freedom.

Notes

1. '59% of Working Women do not make their own decisions: Survey', *Livemint*, 12 October 2022. https://www.livemint.com/money/personal-finance/59-working-women-do-not-make-their-own-financial-decisions-survey-11665555051026.html

2

Lessons from the Pandemic

We Are Not Invincible

And yet we believe that we are. Economists define this staunch belief that bad things happen only to *other people* as the 'Optimism Bias'. Whether it's losing money in the stock market, getting laid off from your job, getting divorced, getting into an accident, having a health emergency, or even sudden death—the optimism bias ensures that we don't see ourselves in any of these situations. We expect good things to happen to us, even if logic and rationality suggests otherwise.

Optimism is not a bad thing. I am an optimist. In my mind, optimism is a necessary companion for life. But not for your family's finances.

Are You Prepared for Sudden Death?

When you're young and doing well—with your career, your health, your relationships—sudden death is not a scenario that's playing in your mind (and it shouldn't be either). But if there is one lesson from the pandemic that's worth tattooing on your brain, it's that shit can hit the proverbial fan when you least expect it to.

The COVID-19 pandemic serves as a grim reminder of this. 5,00,000 Indians—and this is the official count[1]—lost their lives during the pandemic. More than 1,00,000 children were orphaned, left to fend for themselves without any support or security. I am not generalising when I say that most of us will be aware of heartbreaking stories in our own circles, where young folks in their 20s who had to take singular responsibility for families were crippled with both death and debt.

COVID-19 might be over (I hope), but sudden deaths continue to rise with alarming frequency. There has been a significant spike in the number of sudden cardiac arrests among people under the age of 40. Data shows that between the years of 2000 and 2016, the rate of heart attacks in the under-40 age group climbed by 2% every year. Today, 1 in 5 heart attack patients are under the age of 40[2].

Our generation is currently at risk of a slew of lifestyle diseases, (no) thanks to our high-stress, fast-paced lives which force us to deprioritise our health. We continue to believe that we can work on it *tomorrow*. And we continue to believe that bad things 'won't happen to me'. But when has life ever respected our opinion on what it should be?

Who Will ~~Cry~~ Pay the Bills When You Die?

Wow, it just gets more depressing, doesn't it? None of this is to imply that something terrible is going to happen to you tomorrow. But all of this is to definitely ensure that *in the tiny chance that it does, your family isn't left scrambling, financially.*

The good news is that even though bad things don't announce themselves, you can still be prepared for them. And that's where the insurance steps in.

But First—What Is Insurance?

Insurance is the financial equivalent of the 'optional' airbags that you get in cars today. It's tucked away, out of sight, but always there to catch you if things go wrong on the road. And once you've a car with airbags, you don't need to think twice about safety because you *know* it has your back.

Here's the thing about airbags though—you never know when you'll need them. Insurance is no different. You can't predict your claims, which is why insurance is a product that runs on risk. The risk of death, the risk of a car or bike accident, the risk of you going into the hospital, the risk of you missing your flight, or the risk of any other bad thing happening.

And the way it works is fairly straightforward. You—along with other customers—pay the insurance company a token amount called a premium. The insurance company takes your premium in exchange for the guarantee that if (and only if) something bad happens to your car, your bike, your travels, or your health, your bills will be taken care of. This is why you 'claim' your insurance—because you're claiming the guarantee that was promised to you.

So, you buy car insurance to ensure that even if your car gets into an accident, the repairs will be taken care of.

Health insurance, so if you fall sick, your hospitalisation costs will be taken care of. And term life insurance, so if you have an untimely death, your dependents will be taken care of.

If insurance companies are constantly paying claims, how do they make money? Insurance companies run on risk. Not everyone is going to fall sick or crash into each other at the same time. If I were to oversimplify: The premium you and other customers pay is pooled together to fund the claims that have been raised by policyholders who were affected. That's why insurance companies look through your claims with a magnifying glass. They are custodians for all their customers, and it is their responsibility to make sure they're not spending *your* money on fraudulent claims.

Everything You've Wanted to Know about Term Life Insurance (But Didn't Know Who to Ask)

You can't be replaced. But your income can be. That's why we get term life insurance. It's the simplest—and purest—form of insurance.

It provides an assured sum of money to your family in the case of the insured, i.e. your, death. Think of it as a financial love letter for your family—proof that you're looking out for them, even if you're not physically there.

Term life insurance may not have been as popular as its widely peddled siblings, the Endowment life insurance plan or the Annuity life insurance plans, but is probably the most efficient form of life insurance. The main difference between term life insurance and any other form of life insurance is that term life insurance provides a sum assured ***only*** in the event of death, whereas the other plans will give you a 'return' after a certain time period.

Wait, So I Pay and I Don't Get Anything in Return?

Yes. With term life insurance, what you're paying for is a guarantee. A guarantee that *if* anything happens to you, your family is going to be taken care of. If nothing happens to you, all you get is the satisfaction of having made good financial decisions when you were younger.

It's this lack of 'return' that often pushes people away from term life insurance and makes them opt for endowment and annuity plans instead. The only problem is that the latter are often inefficient investments (more on this as the chapter progresses).

But what you need to know is that term life insurance is the most affordable way to ensure a large coverage (i.e, money that will be paid out in case of death) for your family. Often times, the kind of coverage you'd be able to get with term insurance—especially when you buy it at an early age—is 10-12 times what you'd get with an endowment plan.

But First: Who Is Term Life Insurance For?

Listen, not everyone needs term life insurance. Get it only if:

- ⇨ You're the only earning member in the family, or the member with the higher earning power

⇨ You have young children who will need money later in their lives for higher education/pursuing their vocation

⇨ You have parents/siblings who are dependent on your income

How Do I Calculate My Term Insurance Cover?

Okay, so you know you need term life insurance, but how much term insurance do you need? What is the amount you should insure yourself for?

Remember: Term insurance is a replacement for your income. So the coverage you opt for should ideally represent the income that your family will lose in case something happens to you. Here's what you need to account for when you're calculating it:

1. Your age: Your age plays a vital role in determining the amount of money you should insure yourself for. While premiums are cheaper for younger people, families and dependents have so much more to lose in case of a tragedy.

Common wisdom requires you to insure yourself for 10 times your annual income. But when you are young, remember that your potential to earn more money is also greater. So if you're in the 18-35 age group, look to insure yourself for 30X your current annual income.

This way you are also covering the money you would have earned through the years. The 35-55 age group is when a lot of crucial financial decisions are made, especially with respect to children (if any) and retirement, so 20X of current annual income should cover your base, especially if you already have existing investments. 10X of current annual income applies for age 55+.

2. Your dependents: The number of people who are dependent on you for financial support will also determine the amount of money you need to insure yourself for.

If you support both your parents as well as your partner's parents, for example, you will have to revise your estimates upwards. An upward revision should also be considered if you have young children. If you have very few dependents, it might be tempting to insure yourself for less, but that is not advisable. It is always better to err on the side of caution!

3. Your financial background and debt: If you have debt or plan to take debt, your term insurance cover must include the amount of debt you have taken/plan to take. Including debt in your term insurance cover takes the pressure off your family to repay them. They can use the money to focus on their needs versus extinguishing old debt. Consider your background and any future plans you may have committed to as well. You might not consider buying a house now, but is it something you intend to do in a few years? Future plans are especially fuzzy when you're younger. So do consider them when you are arriving at your term insurance cover.

Ultimately, your insurance policy is only as good as your insurance cover. While there are a few basic rules, your cover depends entirely on your and your dependents' needs! While it is morbid to contemplate death, having term insurance, especially in these unpredictable times, will go a long way in preventing a financial crisis for your family.

3 Things to Watch Out for When Buying Term Insurance

1. A critical illness rider: It's not just death that can result in a loss of your income. Sometimes, severe accidents or a critical illness can also ring a financial death-knell on your family, especially if you're the primary breadwinner. So, adding a critical illness rider (or add-on) to your policy will ensure that your family is financially protected.

2. Term Insurance is time bound: The purpose of term insurance is to ensure your dependents are protected in case of an untimely death. But as you get older, clear your debts, attain your financial planning goals, and ready yourself for retirement, chances are that your family and debt obligations are taken care of. So you'd really have no need for term insurance post the age of 65.

Today, there are insurance products called 'whole life' term insurance that offer you term insurance up to the age of 99! But you really don't need it—and the last thing you want to do in your 70s is spend your pension on insurance that you don't really need.

3. No, you don't need your premium to be returned: Some term insurance plans come with a feature called 'return of premium', where, after you pay premiums up to say, the age of 65, you'll have the premiums you paid 'returned' to you by way of a monthly payment, over the course of 15-

20 years. This sounds great, except these policies are much more expensive compared to pure protection.

And that brings us to another important thing.

Don't Be Greedy for Poor Returns—Why Life Insurance Should Be Optimised for Protection and Not Returns

'Life Insurance' is pretty jumbled for those of us in India. After the License Raj of the 60s and 70s, followed by the political turbulence of the 80s, it was only in 1991 that our economy took its first steps into becoming the vibrant landscape that it is today. And it took till 1999, when the Insurance Regulatory & Development Authority of India (IRDAI) was set up, to open up insurance to private players. Until then, insurance was more or less a government monopoly, led by the Life Insurance Corporation of India (LIC) and General Insurance Corporation (GIC).

For those of us born in the late 80s and early 90s, our parents' generation only saw austerity and unrest. They couldn't afford to take risks. And so, LIC became the natural investment option—it was safe, it was a long-term investment, it was backed by the government, and it was considered to be a risk-free way of growing money. You'd pay a premium every year. And at the end of 10, 15, 20 years, you'd be promised (what looked like) a handsome return.

Except when you did the math, the returns were in single digits and often times lower than the price rise that was happening on ground.

Wake Up Babe, It's Not 1993 Anymore

The good news is that today we have way more options when it comes to investment that can guarantee future-proof returns. LIC's growth, and the growth of 'insurance investment', was spurred on by the absence of alternatives for the middle class. The product on paper sounds perfect—you are protected AND you get a return. But closer examination reveals that you receive neither.

The Money You Pay; the Money You Get

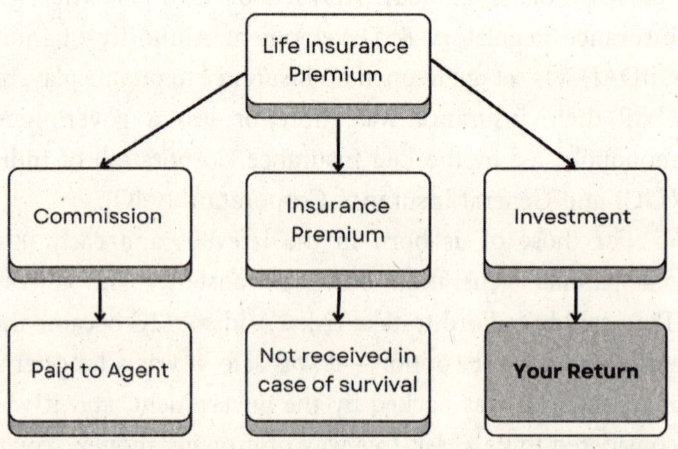

When you pay life insurance (investment) premiums, you're paying for multiple components.

There's one part that will be invested, one part that will go towards actual insurance, and one (big) part that will go to the agent who sold it to you, as commission. The investment and commission components are also subject to GST.

So if you're paying ₹100 as your premium, it's only around ₹50 that's actually being invested to give you a return!

One could argue that you're also getting 'protection' by way of the insurance. But if you look at the sum assured that you'll get in these plans, they're hardly sufficient.

Let's take an example of an endowment or traditional life insurance policy. Assume the policy wants you to pay ₹1,16,000 per annum (roughly ₹9,500 a month) with a sum assured of ₹25,00,000 at the end of the policy period. And let's say the policy period is 20 years. This is standard premium as far as endowment policies are concerned. The insurance cover is likely to be 125% of Sum Assured, which works out to ₹31 lakh.

If the policy states that you have to pay the premium for 15 years, you would have paid ₹17,40,000 by the end of it.

What is the return?

You get the sum assured of ₹25,00,000, a (usually guaranteed) bonus of around 3% of sums assured, which is ₹1,25,000, and a survival bonus of ₹20,00,000, all adding up to ₹46,00,000. It could be more, it could be less, but this is the whereabouts of what you'll receive. On the face of it, it looks like a fab deal. You've nearly tripled your money.

BUT if you had separated your insurance and investments, meaning you buy a pure term insurance for a lower amount and invest the rest in products of your choice, the end result would look very different.

Let me explain:

A term insurance cover of ₹1 crore for a healthy

30-year-old person is ₹25,000 per annum in 2024. That's ₹2,000 a month.

If you can spend ₹9500 on insurance premium, you can split your insurance of ₹2000 and invest the remaining ₹7,500 in an aggressive mutual fund for 15 years. At the end of 15 years, assuming the fund returns 15% year on year, you would've received ₹46,00,000 at the end of year 15 (and not year 20!).

And if you'd kept at it for 5 more years, you'd have landed with a crore. That's a big difference.

DON'T FALL FOR THIS

ULIP and traditional life insurance agents will tell you that these products will give 10-12% returns. This return is on the part that's invested, not on the premium that's paid by you. Ask them instead for the returns on the premium you will pay.

Don't fall for the 'tax saving' either. If you are a salary earner, you're likely paying tax under the 'new regime' which has no special deductions for products like this. Even if you're filing tax in the old regime, there are a number of other tax-friendly investments (like NPS) which qualify.

All of this is to say: If your family is dependent on your income, and you want to ensure that they're always going to be protected, get term insurance. It's the most cost-effective way to ensure they will be. If you want to invest to earn returns, there are tens of thousands of other options for you to explore today.

Don't go for an insurance-linked product.

Health Is (Capable of Destroying) Wealth

One of the biggest lessons that the pandemic taught us (apart from the unpredictability of life), is that yes, health is wealth, but bad health is capable of destroying wealth. Millions of Indians had their family savings wiped out during the pandemic, with many piling up debt and turning to online crowdfunding platforms for aid. Between April and June 2021, 40% of the 4,500 COVID-19 campaigns on the crowdfunding platform, Ketto, were for hospitalisation costs[3].

Indians pay about 63% of their medical expenses out of pocket. It might be alright for a smaller treatment, but when emergencies arrive, hospitalisation costs can put you in ruin. The average cost per day of staying in an ICU is around ₹55,000 in a metro city. Critical care hospitalisation bills, especially for prolonged treatment were reported to be between ₹30 to ₹50 lakh.[4]

India also has one of the highest healthcare inflation rates in the world at 14%. What this number means is that with each passing year, the same treatments will be 14% more expensive. A heart surgery costing ₹3 lakh today could cost ₹6.5 lakh in 6 years. And this doesn't include the cost of medicines, the cost of your room, and other miscellaneous expenses that rack up during hospitalisation.

If you think 6 years is a long time, let me remind you that the pandemic was 5 years ago.

Don't Sleep on Health Insurance

While our public healthcare system—with its incomplete insurance and understaffed health facilities—will take time to correct and arrive at a certain shape, we need to protect our finances with health insurance.

Did you know that only 3 out of 100 Indians have adequate health insurance? While it was a fairly niche product before the pandemic, it is non-negotiable today. And while most of us are ready to buy health insurance, the process of buying health insurance makes us procrastinate, or give up altogether. It's not straightforward, often involves an entire dictionary of terms and conditions, and isn't cheap.

More Is More

When you're buying health insurance, don't skimp on coverage—or the value you're insuring yourself for. Medical costs are only going to increase, and—speaking from experience—a single ICU visit can wipe out your savings. So, it's prudent to go for as much coverage as you can afford. Today, there are plans that offer 'unlimited' coverage, but I'd recommend a minimum of ₹25 lakh if you're staying in a metro city in India.

If you're buying for your family (spouse and kids), get a family floater policy with large coverage, so that even if, god forbid, all 3 of you end up in the hospital for different reasons, there's enough room in the policy to absorb the costs comfortably.

The Health Insurance Jargon Guide

There are plenty of health insurance options in the market right now. But what is right for you? In order to find the policy that's *just right*, you need to decode a number of terms and conditions that aren't one-size-fits-all.

Here's a table on the next page you can refer to.

What I Learned after Working in Insurance for 3 Years

I have been at the helm of a leading insurance company's content and social media efforts for 3 years. Apart from the agonies of the algorithm, here's what I learned—and what I believe you should know—about insurance.

- ⇨ **Insurance Is Not for Planned Events:** Insurance is a product that you buy to protect yourself in case of an unforeseen mishap. An unpredictable event. When you buy insurance to 'cover' for a treatment you know you're going to take in a few months' time, you've either misunderstood the purpose of insurance, or worse, believe that you can get away with misusing the company's trust. Insurance companies are legally bound to ensure that the policy holders' money is not misused in anyway. The claims they pay come out of our premiums, after all. So it's necessary for them to ensure that they're not using up our money for pre-

Term	Meaning	Pros	Cons	What it means for you
Waiting Period	Initial period during which claims cannot be made	Ensures long-term policyholders benefit	Delays coverage for pre-existing conditions	Buying when you're young & healthy and don't have any conditions will ensure no/minimal waiting periods
Pre-existing Disease	Any health issue you had before buying the policy	Coverage included after a waiting period	Long waiting period (often 2-4 years)	
Co-payment	Percentage of claim amount you pay, and the insurer pays the rest	Reduces premium costs	Increases out-of-pocket expenses during claims	Buy a co-pay policy ONLY if you're confident that you'll be able to foot a part of the bill.
Sub-limits	Caps on specific expenses (e.g., room rent, ICU charges)	Keeps premiums affordable	Limits full coverage for high-cost treatments	Hospitalizations and charges aren't predictable. Ideally get a policy without sub-limits
Exclusions	Medical conditions/treatments not covered by the policy	Transparent; helps manage expectations	Important treatments (e.g., pregnancy) may not be covered	Look for policies with minimal exclusions. Childbirth/pregnancy is a very common one.
Network Hospitals	Hospitals with tie-ups for cashless claims	Cashless facility, faster claim process	Limited to specific hospitals; not universal	The wider the hospital network, the better
No Claim Bonus (NCB)	Discount or increased coverage for claim-free years	Rewards healthy policyholders	Can be lost if a claim is made	If your treatment is significantly cheaper than NCB, you're better off paying for it vs claiming.

Term	Meaning	Pros	Cons	What it means for you
Daycare Procedures/OPD	Coverage for treatments that don't require 24-hour hospitalization	Covers common minor procedures	Limited to listed procedures	Check what's covered and what's not. Most policies DON'T cover dental procedures.
Pre/Post-Hospitalization Expenses	Covers expenses before/after hospital stay within specific days	Provides coverage for related treatment costs	Limited time period (e.g., 30/60 days)	This is very useful is you were admitted for a prolonged illness.
Restoration Benefit	Reinstates sum insured if fully used once in a year	Extends coverage for multiple claims	Usually for unrelated claims, not the same illness	Restoration benefits are particularly useful for family floater policies
Room Rent Limit	Cap on daily room rent in case of hospitalization	Keeps premium low	Higher room charges mean out-of-pocket expenses	Ensure that your policy doesn't have room rent limits. You don't have control over available rooms/might prefer a larger room. You don't want limits here.
Ambulance Cover	Covers ambulance charges during emergencies	Financial relief for emergency transport	May have limits on coverage amount	Ensure that your policy has a basic cover for ambulance charges.
Lifetime Renewability	Option to renew policy for life without new medical checks	Continuous coverage, even at old age	None, but not all policies offer this	Enquire on lifetime renewability at the time of buying.
Cashless Claims	Facility where insurer settles bills directly with hospital	Convenient; less paperwork for the insured	Limited to network hospitals	Wider network will ensure greater chance of cashless claims

planned procedures. This means that at the time of claims, there is a rigorous background check that's done with the hospital to understand how and why the patient was diagnosed, and their history. Many folks believe that it's possible to 'hide' their pre-existing conditions by just changing doctors or hospitals, but insurance companies also have doctors who are on their payroll to cross verify claims and ensure that policyholders aren't taking the company for a ride. So when it comes to insurance, honesty is not just the best policy, it's also the only policy.

- ⇨ **Claim Your Youth Discount:** When it comes to insurance, your age is your superpower. Younger applicants are considered to be low risk, which means that you'll get top tier policies at a far more economical rate than you would in your 40s (which is when people usually realise they need insurance). Younger applicants are also exempted, usually, from the rigorous medical testing that older folks are required to undertake. So, buying health and term insurance when you're young is a very smart decision.
- ⇨ **Your Corporate Policy Is Probably Not Enough:** If you work in a corporate set up, you've likely been set up with health insurance. Corporate health insurance is great because you do get a wider range of benefits, including the ability to be able to cover your parents (for whom getting health insurance

might otherwise be hard). That said, even the best corporate health insurance policies don't go beyond 5 lakh in coverage. Two nights in an ICU can set you back by this amount, leave alone the cost of procedures. What's more, even if you stay healthy, getting health insurance becomes an expensive affair as you get older. So, getting standalone health insurance—either as a fresh policy or getting a cheaper, 'top up' policy that kicks in when you run out of your corporate policy—becomes necessary.

⇨ **Don't Forget the 8 Year Rule:** Did you know that your insurer is *obligated* to pay your claims if you pay your premiums on time for 8 years? The IRDAI refers to these 8 years as the 'moratorium' period and states that: 'After the expiry of Moratorium Period no health insurance claim shall be contestable except for proven fraud and permanent exclusions specified in the policy contract.'[5] While sub-limits, co-pay conditions, deductibles etc., will continue to function as per the policy, your claim *has* to be paid out. This is a rule that's also insurer agnostic. Let's say you bought a policy with company A, paid premiums for 3 years, and now want to switch to company B. If you port your policy with company A to company B, your moratorium period continues to accumulate with company B. So make sure you don't skip your policy renewal dates to ensure that your moratorium period continues.

Uncle Vs Direct—Which Route Do You Take?

Who do you buy your insurance policies from? Irrespective of whether it's for your car or for your life, there's always an agent available to sell it for you. But these days, with the internet and comparison engines, it's never been easier to buy a policy directly from the insurance company. But how do you know which decision is best?

Commission Vs Conviction

When you buy directly from the insurance company, your premium prices will be SIGNIFICANTLY cheaper. That's because when you buy from the agent, there is an aspect of commission that's loaded into the premium you pay *every single year*. On the other hand, having an agent will mean that you have a single point of contact any time you need to make a claim. You let the agent uncle know and he will liaise with the insurance company to do his best to push your claim through.

That said, going through an agent makes sense when the agent in question is someone you can catch hold of even a decade later. If you don't have an insurance uncle in your life who visits you every year, sends you sweets on Diwali, and flowers on birthdays, you're almost always better off buying directly from the insurance company.

Agent-led Claims Aren't Always Successful

One of the common misconceptions around buying insurance from agents is that they'll be able to pull your claims through. This isn't always the case—if it were, all insurance companies would have a 100% claim settlement ratio, a number you should inspect before you buy the policy. While an agent can reduce your load during a stressful time (like an accident or hospitalisation), they *cannot* guarantee your claim.

Insurance Companies Aren't What They Used to Be—In A Good Way

As technology and data science make leaps and bounds, insurance companies are now more aware than ever of the power of customer data, which can enable them to predict risk better and offer better services. It is in their interest to ensure that the relationship that a customer has with them is under *their* control versus an agent's. So there have been efforts to ensure that customer communications are more efficient and empathetic.

All of this is to say that there is no right or wrong approach. It's simply the one that you're more comfortable with.

Keep a Record

Among the more unpleasant revelations that emerged from the pandemic was how little families knew about *their own finances.* It was quite telling—families' CAs knew more about where the household's savings were than the partner. The pandemic amplified the pain of running from pillar to post while battling grief, especially in many cases where the CAs were also in the hospital.

You can prevent a great deal of heart ache for your family

if you just keep a record of your financial information. It's very easy to have a privately shared or password-protected spreadsheet that can be updated regularly.

Here's what your finance master sheet needs to have:

1. *Your Identity Documents:* PAN Card copy, Aadhar Card copy, Income Tax login credentials
2. *Your Bank Account(s):* Account number, bank name, branch, IFSC code, Net Banking credentials
3. *Your Demat account(s):* Account number, login credentials, depository name
4. *Your Insurance Documents*: Policy name, number, sum assured, annual premiums, agent's number (if you used one)
5. *Asset Register*: Details of large assets in your name—if you have plots of land, houses in other locations, bank lockers etc, put everything down here

The above list is only suggestive and I'd highly recommend you spend some time with a spreadsheet to create a format that works for you. You can even sit with your partner or parent and help them understand it as well.

It's Bad Luck!

We are a superstitious culture. And often times, the very act of being prepared for an emergency is equated to inviting one. But it's time we took a pragmatic lens to life's unpredictabilities and ensure that our families will always be protected. Bad things can happen to any one of us. But worse things happen to those who don't prepare themselves for it.

Lessons from the Pandemic—The TL; DR

Here's what I want you to take away from this chapter:

Bad Things CAN Happen to Us

If COVID-19 taught us anything, it's that life doesn't care about our plans, and yet, we continue to run on optimism. Being optimistic is great—but not when it comes to your family's finances. Ask yourself: if the worst happened, how prepared would your family be?

Term Insurance, Because Simple Is Beautiful

Instead of chasing complicated life-insurance plans that promise 'returns', opt for term insurance. It's affordable, straightforward, and there to ensure your family is financially secure if something happens to you.

Health Is Literally Wealth

Hospital bills during the pandemic wiped out families' savings. With India's healthcare inflation rising at 14% annually, an ICU visit alone can crush your finances. Health insurance isn't just 'nice to have'—it's non-negotiable.

Choose a plan with high coverage (at least ₹25 lakh if you live in a metro), so no matter what hits, you can focus on getting better, instead of worrying about your bank balance.

Claim Your 'Youth Discount'

The younger you are, the cheaper your premiums. Insurance companies love low-risk clients, and that's exactly what you are in your 20s and 30s. Secure your plan early before health issues—or age—up your premium.

Keep Track of Everything

The pandemic exposed how unprepared many of us are. Share a simple spreadsheet with all your important financial details—insurance policies, bank accounts, investments, etc., with your loved ones. It'll save them a lot of stress.

Insurance Agents vs. DIY

Agents can help during claims, but they also take a cut. If you're tech-savvy, buying insurance directly from the company can save you money.

Don't Fall for Outdated Advice

Traditional insurance plans were survival tools for our parents' generation—they're not the best investment anymore. Today, splitting your insurance needs (term plan) and investment needs (mutual funds or SIPs) gets you far better returns.

Preparation Isn't Jinxing

Planning for worst-case scenarios is an undoubtedly smart thing to do. Storms don't check if you're ready before they strike.

Notes

1. Statista Research Department, 'Total number of novel coronavirus (COVID-19) deaths in the Asia-Pacific region as of April 2024, by country or territory', 18 September 2024. https://www.statista.com/statistics/1104268/apac-covid-19-deaths-by-country/
2. Varsha Vats, 'What Is the Reason for Increased Heart attacks in Young People', *NDTV,* 29 September 2023. https://www.ndtv.com/health/what-is-the-reason-for-increased-number-of-heart-attacks-in-young-people-2715027
3. AP, 'Pandemic leaves Indians mired in massive debts', *The Economic Times*, 26 July 2021. https://economictimes.indiatimes.com/news/india/pandemic-leaves-indians-mired-in-massive-medical-debts/articleshow/84757111.cms
4. Sarfaraz Ahmed, '10-fold rise in critical care cost made treatment expensive', *The Times of India*, 30 October 2023. https://timesofindia.indiatimes.com/city/nagpur/10-fold-rise-in-critical-care-cost-made-treatment-expensive/articleshow/104810478.cms
5. IRDAI Guidelines on standardisation of general terms and clauses in health insurance policy contracts: https://irdai.gov.in/document-detail?documentId=394691

3

My First Job

My first salary as an articled assistant in a chartered accountant's office was the princely sum of ₹1,000 a month. Lest you think this was in the 80s, it was actually in 2007. CA stipends—unless you worked in a Big 4 accounting firm like PriceWaterhouseCoopers, Ernst & Young, Deloitte, or KPMG—were infamous for their insignificance. The bar was already low, but our stipends were lower. Although the amount was a joke, the first time it got credited to my bank account, it felt monumental. I was earning. This money was mine. These stipend credits were my first taste of financial independence. It gave me a glimmer of all the potential that my life could have as my career progressed.

I've been working for 18 years now. I've seen very many things during my work life, but what I haven't seen are peers discussing their paychecks. It's the white elephant in the room. The black box in our career jets. And while it's not easy or fair to get people to talk about the specifics of how much money they're making, it is important to talk about the components of our salaries in a more transparent way. After all, the very landscape of work that we navigate today, whether we're just entering the job market or navigating a transition, has changed drastically with the rise of the Great Indian Startup.

Knowledge of how salaries work—whether you talk about it or not—isn't just going to help your finances. It's going to fuel your career.

Your CTC Is Different from the Money that Actually Gets Credited in Your Bank Account

One of the first things to understand is the difference between your 'Cost to Company' or CTC and your take-home pay, that is the money that actually gets credited in your bank account.

Your CTC is what the company is spending on you, as an employee. This includes not just your salary but also benefits, bonuses, employer contributions to provident fund (PF), and other perks.

Your take-home salary, on the other hand, is what gets credited to your bank account. This is usually lower than your CTC because some components of the CTC—like PF contributions, cab or bus allowances, food allowances—in some ways, are not directly paid to you. The deductions and taxes are not directly paid to you but go towards your future savings and obligations.

Example: If your CTC is ₹12,00,000 per annum, don't expect your monthly paycheck to be ₹1,00,000 (₹12,00,000 ÷ 12). Your monthly take-home could be significantly lower after deductions like income tax, PF, etc.

The Components of Your Salary

Your salary isn't just a single number—it comprises multiple components, each with different tax implications. But with the new income tax regime and the proposed Income-tax Bill, 2025, many of these components no longer work the way they used to. So, it's likely that if you've been in the workforce for a while, you'll be seeing an overhaul in the way your salary is structured.

Here's what you need to know.

Basic Pay

This is the foundation of your salary, typically making up 40-50% of your total CTC. It serves as the base for calculating other components like bonuses and employer contributions. Basic pay is fully taxable under both the old and new tax regimes.

What's changed? Nothing has changed in how basic pay is structured, but under the new tax regime, you no longer have deductions like HRA or Section 80C investments to lower your taxable income. This means that the higher your basic salary, the greater the tax you'll have to pay.

House Rent Allowance (HRA)

HRA was one of the most useful tax exemptions for salaried employees who rented homes. Under the old tax regime, a significant portion of rent expenses could be deducted from taxable income, particularly for those living in metro cities.

What's changed? The new tax regime does not allow HRA deductions. If you choose the new regime, your

HRA is fully taxable. If your employer allows flexibility in structuring your salary, consider negotiating for a higher basic pay instead of an HRA component, as it simplifies tax calculations.

Special Allowances

These include allowances for conveyance, phone bills, fuel reimbursements, meal vouchers, and other benefits. Under the old regime, many of these allowances were partially or fully tax-exempt, provided you submitted proof of expenses (these proofs are what HR dutifully emails you for every January!).

What's changed? Under the new tax regime, all special allowances are fully taxable. This means that reimbursements and allowances that previously offered tax savings will now be treated as part of your taxable income.

If a large portion of your salary was structured as allowances, it may be time to renegotiate your CTC. Without the tax exemptions, it is often more beneficial to receive a higher basic salary than a taxable allowance.

Performance Bonuses and Incentives

Bonuses are typically tied to individual performance, company profits, or both. Some employers spread bonuses across multiple months to reduce the tax burden for employees.

What's changed? Bonuses were always taxable, and they remain so under the new regime. However, since there are fewer deductions available, your bonus could push you into a higher tax bracket more easily. This makes it even more important to understand your employer's bonus structure and whether you can optimise it.

What Salary Earners Need to Know About the New Tax Regime

- The new tax regime continues to be optional. High earners (starting from those earning above ₹60LPA), with deductions like PF, Health Insurance, NPS, and loans, are better off with the old regime. If you've just entered the work force, the new regime offers far more benefits.
- Standard deductions have increased to ₹75,000, but all other deductions (including HRA, 80C, and 80D) are no longer applicable.
- HRA and Special Allowances are now fully taxable with no exemptions.
- Reimbursements for expenses like fuel or phone bills no longer offer tax benefits.
- Bonuses remain taxable, and without deductions, they could increase your overall tax liability.
- Your salary structure matters more than ever—negotiating for a higher basic pay instead of allowances can maximise take-home salary.
- If you're switching to the new regime and your CTC still includes allowances that no longer provide tax relief, it may be time to have a discussion with HR about restructuring your salary.

The new tax regime is designed for simplicity, but that does not mean you shouldn't optimise it to your advantage.

You'll Be a Man, My Son

Said Rudyard Kipling, in 'If'. While I don't have philosophical advice, I do have a few points on the financial habits you'd need to pick up once you start earning. These are non-negotiables, so consider them to be what you need for financial housekeeping.

You Need a Budget

When it comes to getting in control of your money, budgeting is the first step. But what is a budget? A budget is nothing but a financial plan. Knowing how to create a budget can help you identify what you're spending on and make your savings process more efficient. Budgeting is often considered to be some kind of restriction that you must place on your finances. But it's not about restricting as much as it is about recording. Having and maintaining a budget will help you identify what you're spending your money on. This way, you can understand where the gaps in your spending are and come up with solutions specifically for those areas.

Budgeting is a lot like journaling, in that it requires a consistent commitment. While the initial drawing of tables and going through numbers can be exciting, you will have to come back to your budget regularly if you want to make it stick. So, think about how you can make this consistency easy. Maybe you'd be comfortable carrying your budget everywhere, so you can record your expenses as and when they occur. If so, put it on your phone. Or maybe you'd prefer setting aside 15 minutes every evening to put your expenses together. Zero in on what works for you and commit to the process.

Start by tracking your expenses daily. It's kind of like having a food diary. When you make yourself aware and start spending consciously, you will start seeing changes in the way that you spend.

Build a Habit of Saving

No one's asking you to immediately put away 50% of your salary in savings (although if you're living with your parents during the early years of your career, you should). But what you need is to set up a habit and automate your savings. Investments shouldn't be an afterthought. Start small—maybe 10% of your salary every month in an investment of your choice. Today, fintechs allow you to set up auto-debits that ensure the money gets invested, so you don't have to remember to make the investment each time. Revisit the amount you're investing every 6-12 months. When it's automated, there's never a question of 'if' you're saving. Only how much.

Pay Yourself First

When you're automating your savings, make sure it's very close to pay day. I like sharing this equation whenever I speak to folks in their 20s about saving. If Salary—Expenses = Savings, then you're paying yourself last. If Salary—

Savings = Expenses, then you're paying yourself first. So, pay yourself first. Every time you do, future you will be grateful that you put them first.

Item 1 on the Agenda: Emergency Fund

Before you get sucked into mutual funds and the *hajaar* options that are out there for you to invest in, build an emergency fund. An emergency fund is your financial life jacket. The wooden door that kept Kate Winslet afloat in *Titanic*. It is an easily accessible sum of money that can help you at any time.

A basic emergency fund covers 3 months of expenses. Think about it this way—if you were to lose all your income tomorrow, for whatever reason, how much would you need to get through 3 months? You can add up all your expenses for a month—namely, rent, utilities, healthcare, internet, groceries, subscriptions, and anything else that you might consider essential. Then you multiply it by 3 to arrive at the end amount.

An easier calculation (but a more difficult target) would be to multiply your current income by three. This will take longer to save, but will provide a greater cushion.

The idea of putting together 3 months of expenses or income can be daunting. But if you can be slightly aggressive with the way that you save, or try budgeting to cut down on your unnecessary expenses, you can reach your goal faster than you think.

Your emergency fund should be in a place that's easily accessible. Think of a situation where you might have to produce money for a hospital advance, for example. Your bank account is one place to hold it in. But if you're afraid that you might end up spending it, you could park it in an FD.

Learn to Say No

Working is never as simple as just showing up to the office, doing the work, and leaving. It's almost tribal in its expectations—you have to indulge in community rituals like coffee machine gossip, clothing of a certain stature (especially if you work in more conservative sectors like finance) or if you're in tech, after-work beers.

With the exception of gossip, none of these pursuits are cheap. Our progress at work, after all, is rarely determined by the actual work that we do, but the perception that others have of the work we do. And if we are to build a positive perception, certain types of *kharchas* are inevitable.

But there will come a point when peer-pressure-led spends—whether it's on a shiny gadget, or endless pub crawls every week, or a wardrobe that's way out of your budget—will come to bite your savings in the behind.

So, the biggest financial skill you can pick up in your 20s, is the ability to say no.

And no, this doesn't mean becoming a party pooper! Participate, but know your limits. Your financial well-being is your business—because, no one else at the table is losing sleep over how you're funding your lifestyle.

Show up, but show out smartly.

Yeah, It Can All Be a Bit Much

The constitution of India recognises any individual to be an adult when they reach 18 years of age. But when do you *feel* like an adult? When do you grow up in the ways that you want to? In the ways that you're expected to?

Life and all its paperwork don't hit most of us until we're in our mid-20s—all privilege disclaimers apply. I recently conducted a very scientific survey (by running a poll on Twitter) to better understand when people felt like they'd finally climbed, or at least had embarked on their climb, to Mount Adulthood. Of the 780 odd people who voted, 58% responded that they'd truly started feeling like adults—self-sufficient and responsible—when they moved out of their parent's houses.

And that makes sense because when you live by yourself, a fair share of responsibility does come your way, even if it's not necessarily money related. But what if you never get the opportunity to have that experience? What if you've never had to be responsible for yourself? More importantly, what happens when you find yourself responsible for someone else before you get the chance to be responsible for yourself? What happens then?

The good news is that self-sufficiency is not as hard as it's perceived to be. The reason we get errand paralysis or feel that it becomes 'too much' is because we tend to take everything on at the same time—bills, debt, investments, budgeting, insurance, tax. I mean, of course you're going to be overwhelmed. Of course you're going to want a holiday.

The key to success with owning your finances—and

consequently, your life—is to take things on one at a time. Pick one area, get it right, and then move on to the next one. And then the next one. And the next one…and just like that, you'll get where you need to be.

Your Sweat, Their Equity

On 22 September 2021, the B2B SAAS giant, Freshworks, went public in the US, becoming the first Indian company to be listed on NASDAQ. For those of us from Chennai—where Freshworks was headquartered—this was big news. Gireesh Mathrubootham, the founder of Freshworks, was well known for being unabashed about his ambition. In an interview with *The Economic Times* in 2015, he famously said, 'When I started the company I told my wife that I am not starting a company for me to buy a BMW, I am starting a company so that all my employees can buy BMWs.'

And when Freshworks went public, that's more or less what happened. Techies from Chennai who'd worked with Freshworks for years found themselves to be dollar millionaires—and Chennai's luxury car demand was never the same again!

The great Freshworks IPO story is just one in the ever-increasing list of 'new age' companies going public and enabling their employees who'd stuck around to earn serious wealth, thanks to ESOPs.

What Are ESOPs? How Do They Work?

An Employee Stock Option Plan (ESOP) is exactly what it sounds like—a plan where your company offers you the option to buy shares in the company at a fixed, discounted price (called the exercise price or strike price) in the future. If your company's valuation skyrockets, this can mean huge profits when you eventually sell these shares.

Here's how it works:

- ⇨ Your company offers you X number of shares at a strike price of, say, ₹1 per share.
- ⇨ A few years later, your company's shares are worth ₹1,000 each.
- ⇨ If you exercise your option (i.e., buy the shares at ₹1), you can sell them at ₹1,000 and make a cool profit of ₹999 per share.

But…there's a catch.

You don't get all your shares on day 1. ESOPs typically come with a vesting schedule—a timeline that determines when you earn the right to exercise your stock options.

A common vesting schedule looks like this:

- ⇨ **Cliff period:** Most companies have a 1-year cliff. This means you need to stay at the company for at least a year before any shares vest.
- ⇨ **Monthly or yearly vesting:** After the cliff, you vest a portion of your shares monthly or annually. For example, if you have 4,000 shares over 4 years, you may vest 1,000 shares each year.

This structure benefits the company (by retaining you) and ensures that employees don't bounce after securing their shares. If you're considering quitting at the 11-month mark, you might forfeit all the shares you're entitled to! So, read that vesting schedule carefully, and remember: no pain, no gain.

So, When Do You Cash Out?

The moment of truth for any ESOP holder is the liquidity event—this could be an IPO (Initial Public Offering) where shares are listed on the stock market or an internal acquisition where the company buys its shares back from you.

But until this liquidity event happens, your shares are essentially paper money. You might see 6-digit figures in your ESOP allocation, but unless your company reaches a successful exit (via IPO or acquisition), that paper value doesn't mean much.

Why Isn't Everyone Just Getting Paid in ESOPs?

Here's a sobering reality check: Around 90% of startups fail.

Only a small percentage ever achieve the kind of financial success that results in a big liquidity event. The guys who made crores from Swiggy are the ones who were grinding when the company was just an idea. The ones who took the bet and won. History, after all, only remembers victors. You'll never see headlines about the engineers who spent years waiting for their ESOP windfall, only to see their startup burn out.

This isn't to scare you away from startups—but it's important to manage your expectations. When you accept ESOPs as part of your compensation package, you're betting on the company's future success.

Ask yourself:

1. Do I believe in the leadership's vision?
2. Is the company's product competitive and scalable?
3. How long do I want to work here, realistically?

What to Expect When You're Expecting ESOPs

The number of options you receive is meaningless without knowing the company's valuation or future plans. Here's what you should ask for during negotiations:

- What is the company's latest valuation? This helps you understand the worth of your shares in comparison to what you'll be paying for them.
- What is the vesting schedule? Slow vesting schedules mean that your ESOPs are locked into how long you'll stay there. Annual vesting schedules also mean that you'll have be very strategic about when you plan to leave if the job gets toxic or if you get a better offer. The faster the vesting schedule (quarterly or monthly), the better the ESOP package.
- What is the liquidity timeline? This is a polite way of asking when you'll get to see some money. Asking this question will inform you of what's in the horizon for the company in terms of IPO, or at the very least, in terms of internal liquidity events.

The Double Tax Problem

One of the most frustrating things about ESOPs in India is in how it's taxed—twice.

The first time you're taxed is when you exercise your options. Let's say you're offered 1 share at a strike price of ₹1. And the valuation is ₹1,000. You've essentially made a profit of ₹999. This (notional or imaginary) gain of ₹999 will be taxed as income in the year you exercised your options and bought the shares.

The second time is when you sell the shares. If the market value of your 1 share is ₹2,500, then you'll pay capital gains tax on ₹1,500, that is, the difference between market value (₹2,500) and the share value (₹1,000).

This double taxation is a very sore point and has been debated to no end in corporate circles, but there's no reprieve in sight (yet). Here's hoping I get to rewrite this section soon.

All That Glitters Isn't ESOPs

ESOPs can be life-changing, but they're not a guaranteed jackpot. They're a high-risk, high-reward part of your compensation package that requires careful consideration. And that's why knowing your terms and asking the right questions means you're making an informed choice—not taking a gamble.

Ask for It: Why You Need to Negotiate a Raise

Negotiating your raise is not just about getting a bump in your paycheck—it can also define your future wealth. The (ugly) truth is, for most salaried employees, this is one of the few opportunities we have to meaningfully increase our incomes and set ourselves up for financial security.

Unless you actively learn to advocate for ourselves and

negotiate better, you risk being stuck at a level of income that doesn't match your contributions or your potential. Salaries are supposed to compound, not stagnate.

Don't Be Shy

When it comes to asking for a raise, timing, preparation, and approach are important. After all, your strategy hinges on how long you've been with the company. The folks who've been around for 5 years would focus on loyalty, versus those who've been around for 3, who'd focus on growth, versus the folks who've been around for a year, who'd focus on the immense value they may have added in their first year.

Irrespective of your strategy or experience levels, the most important thing when it comes to salary negotiations is simply to ask. Employees—especially women—need to be able to self-advocate and know how to sell themselves. It's the crying baby, after all, that gets the milk.

Jumping Jobs, Leaping Paychecks

Switching jobs is one of the most effective ways to secure a substantial pay bump. The common wisdom of asking for a 30% hike and data show that job switchers tend to see salary increases between 20-40%, depending on their industry and role. But remember, the percentage depends on various factors like market demand, your skill set, and company budget.

Jumping jobs might give you a fatter increment, but remember that jumping too often can also put you on an

HR hitlist as a flaky resource and ruin future opportunities. So be strategic about when and how you want to make these larger leaps.

Let me also be honest in saying that it's much easier to negotiate with new people than old ones because there's no bias that exists. Make sure you back your ask with research (through platforms like Glassdoor or LinkedIn Salary Insights) and ensure that you're happy with your pay structure before you sign it. The last open spot you have for negotiation when you take on a new job is after you receive your offer but before you sign it. So make sure that you've gone through the fine print before you sign.

The Gender Pay Gap

Let's talk about something no one likes to admit exists but affects nearly every working woman: The gender pay gap.

The numbers are frustrating but not surprising. According to data from the World Economic Forum[1], Indian women only earn ₹40 for every ₹100 that their male counterpart does, even when experience and qualifications are the same. And it gets worse as you climb the ladder—the higher up you go, the wider the gap becomes.

There are plenty of reasons for this, but here are the big ones:

- **Women don't negotiate as often**: We are conditioned to be grateful for what we get, while men are taught to ask for more. A study by Harvard Business Review[2] showed that while 57% of men negotiate their salaries, only 7% of women do. If you take just one thing away from this section, let it be this: ALWAYS negotiate your salary.

- **We are penalised for ambition**: Studies show that when women ask for raises or promotions, they are seen as 'demanding' or 'difficult', while men doing the same are seen as 'assertive' and 'leadership material'. The result? Many women hold back, waiting to be recognised, while their male peers climb faster simply because they ask.
- **Motherhood = Career penalty**: Although India has one of the world's most progressive maternity leave policies (up to 26 weeks of paid leave), the so-called 'motherhood penalty' is real. Many workplaces assume, consciously or unconsciously, that women will take breaks, work fewer hours, or be 'less committed' after having kids. This isn't just sexist—it's economically damaging, because it leads to fewer promotions, fewer raises, and fewer leadership positions for women.
- **Women are overrepresented in lower-paying jobs**: Women tend to dominate fields like HR, teaching, social work, and administration—jobs that, despite requiring significant skill, are paid less than male-dominated fields like tech and finance.
- **Workplaces are built for men**: From networking opportunities (hello, Sunday cricket and after-hours drinks) to how performance is measured, the modern workplace is still largely designed for men. If you're not in the boys' club, you miss out on mentorship, promotions, and big career moves.

So, What Can You Do?

Start by talking about money. The more we normalise salary conversations, the harder it becomes for companies to justify pay gaps. Ask around, research salaries, and know your worth before walking into a negotiation.

Next, negotiate aggressively. Don't accept the first offer. Men negotiate. You should too. If they say no, ask what it would take to reach your number in the next cycle. Make them commit. Finally, document everything! Keep track of your work, wins, and contributions. If your raise doesn't match your impact, bring receipts.

Gender pay gaps don't disappear with time—they disappear when we *demand* better.

Got a Gig?

According to a BCG report[3], India houses nearly 8 million gig professionals or freelancers. 53% of these gig workers will have work in white-collar spaces like IT, recruitment, and education. And as per the Niti Aayog report, 'India's Booming Gig and Platform Economy',[4] the Indian gig workforce is expected to expand to 23.5 million workers by the year 2029-30, which is nearly 3 times the current number.

As workplaces get more demanding, more and more professionals are turning to freelancing, which allows them flexibility and the ability to earn on their terms. Freelancing is particularly friendly for women, who can earn while catering to the needs of their families.

The flipside of freelancing is that the income is never a

steady amount that you'll receive every month, which can make financial planning challenging.

But there are ways to create a financial plan if you're on a variable wage.

Take Stock

To plan for the future, you need to be clear about your present. List down your present bank balances, fixed deposits, credit cards, bills that you're yet to pay, money that you're due to receive, loans that are in your name, property that you own, any investments that you may have made so far and insurance policies that you have taken out in your name. This, of course, is just an indicative list—feel free to add financial details that you may think are necessary and cut out what doesn't apply to you but make the list. It is only when you do, that you'll have a complete idea of the money in your name.

This exercise can be overwhelming if you're doing it for the first time, so if you're finding it difficult, I'd suggest you spread this exercise over the course of a few days. The more you consolidate information, the more confident you'll get with handling your finances.

Create Savings 'Buckets'

When you're a freelancer or self-employed, you don't have the advantage of the pension fund and insurance benefits that your peers with corporate jobs do. The good news is that you can customise your savings plan entirely to suit your needs.

You can create different 'buckets' or categories of savings. You can have a 'retirement bucket', a 'nice things bucket', where you save for specific items that are expensive, like a holiday or new furniture, and so on. It's important to identify categories and separate your savings, so when you do dip into them, the overall structure of your finances is not disturbed. Separating your savings also makes it easy to prioritise where your money needs to go during low-income spells and when you receive a windfall, make sure you save more instead of sticking to the usual amount.

Create a Financial Support System

When you're salaried, there are certain benefits you can take advantage of—health insurance, taking your salary in advance, and support from colleagues in times of emergencies. When you're working as a freelancer, you're quite literally on your own. While everyone has their own emotional support systems, you need to make sure your financial support system is in place. Emergency funds and a solid health insurance plan are non-negotiable.

The Tea on GST

With great flexibility, comes...GST. If you're a freelancer providing services, making more than ₹20 lakh in billing (₹10 lakh for special category states, namely, Arunachal Pradesh, Assam, Jammu and Kashmir, Manipur, Meghalaya, Mizoram, Nagaland, Sikkim, Tripura, Himachal Pradesh, and Uttarakhand), you have to register for GST.

If you provide interstate services—such as working with

clients across state borders—you're required to register for GST, even if your earnings are below ₹20 lakh.

And if you're using an online platform like Upwork or Fiverr to receive payments, then you have to register irrespective of how much you're billing.

Being GST-compliant requires a lot of administrative work. From invoices to returns, you will have to put in extra work to not only get it done, but get it done on time. That said, registering for GST will enable you to claim Input Tax Credit (ITC). Let's say you've paid ₹1,800 in GST on your invoice, but you paid ₹800 in GST on a collar mic that you need for your projects, you'll only have to pay ₹1,000 (1,800–1,000) to the tax man.

This can bring a lot of relief to your tax burden.

My only piece of advice is this: Many freelancers ignore GST thinking that they're 'just starting out'. Ignoring registration requirements could lead to heavy penalties, so it's crucial to assess your financial setup and register if you meet any criteria.

Staying GST-compliant doesn't just keep you out of legal trouble—it helps you stay on top of your finances and keeps your cash flow healthy.

Borrowing Is Harder When You're a Freelancer

Traditionally, lenders prefer salaried employees over freelancers. The stable, predictable income streams are far more attractive for lenders versus freelancers whose incomes fluctuate. It signals to lenders that you carry a greater risk and as a result, you lose negotiating power.

That said, if you can prove that your income is rising year on year, you're more likely to win the favour of the lender.

Freelancing Needs Thought

These days it seems attractive to become a freelancer, especially for folks in the tech and creative fields. The idea that you don't have to be tied down is attractive to anyone, to be honest. But know that the grass is always going to be greener on the other side. Salaried employment promises career growth, career development, and stability that can't be quantified in words. In fact, according to a report published by CIEL[5], a talent management company, 50% of gig workers expressed their interest to pursue full-time employment!

My First Job—The TL; DR

Paychecks Are Awesome

The thrill of earning your first salary, even if it's small, represents a step toward financial independence.

CTC vs. Take-Home Pay

Your Cost to Company (CTC) is the total your employer spends on you, including allowances and benefits. What lands in your bank account is usually much less after taxes, Provident Fund (PF) deductions, and other benefits.

Get the Basics Right

Budgeting and building a savings habit—these are two key financial habits you should pick up the moment you start earning.

Draw Your Lines

From work-appropriate attire to socialising expenses, career growth often comes with financial costs. Learning to set spending boundaries early is crucial to staying financially healthy.

Get Sweaty

ESOPs let employees buy company shares at a discounted price. They can be lucrative if the company succeeds, but they're risky and subject to double taxation.

We're All in Shark Tank

Negotiating your raise or compensation package is key to building long-term wealth. Research salary benchmarks, ask for what you're worth, and read the fine print.

Freelancing Is Never Free

Jumping into freelancing might seem attractive, but flexibility comes with its own pitfalls. Create savings buckets to make sure your goals are met and remember that health insurance is non-negotiable.

Notes

1. BT Desk, 'India on Global Gender Gap Index: Women continue to earn less than men, only Rs 40 for every Rs 100 earned respectively', *Business Today*, 13 June 2024. https://www.businesstoday.in/latest/economy/story/india-on-global-gender-gap-index-disparity-continues-as-women-early-only-rs-40-for-every-rs-100-earned-by-men-433190-2024-06-13
2. Linda Babcock, Sara Laschever, Michele Gelfand, and Deborah Small, 'Nice Girls Don't Ask', *Harvard Business Review*, October 2003. https://hbr.org/2003/10/nice-girls-dont-ask
3. BCG, 'Unlocking the Potential of the Gig Economy in India'. https://media-publications.bcg.com/India-Gig-Economy-Report.pdf
4. NITI Aayog, 'India's Booming Gig and Platform Economy', June 2022. https://www.niti.gov.in/sites/default/files/2022-06/25th_June_Final_Report_27062022.pdf
5. CIEL HR, 'Employment Trends in the Gig Sector in India', June 2023. https://www.cielhr.com/wp-content/uploads/2023/10/Employment-Trends-in-the-Gig-Sector-in-India-2.pdf

Q&A: Shephali Bhatt

Shephali Bhatt is an independent Tech & Culture reporter and researcher, who specialises in human interest features on Tech, Pop Culture, Internet Subcultures, and Media and Entertainment. Her work focuses on chronicling how the internet transforms the way we live, and how corporates adapt to those changing ways. Her work has been published in *The Economic Times, Livemint, Brand Equity,* and more.

1. Making the shift from a full-time job to freelancing can be a financially nerve-wracking decision. What kind of financial safety net should someone have before making the jump from a steady paycheck to freelancing?

You're right. It is nerve-wracking, indeed. And I may not have been able to take that decision if making rent was a huge concern for me, especially in a place like Mumbai. I frankly don't know anyone in the freelance journalism circuit who doesn't have some sort of safety net—their own house, a partner with a stable sustainable income, and so on. That is not to say every freelancer has some safety net, but that it makes it easier to make that decision if you have some, otherwise you're constantly struggling to make rent and that can have an adverse effect on how you feel about being in your line of work.

2. Unlike a salary, freelance income is unpredictable. What financial habits or structures helped you manage cash flow without financial anxiety?

I structured my projects in such a way that I had a big long-term project—that takes care of substantial in-hand income every month. And it allows me to then make up the deficit from other projects. I try to ensure the other projects are non-writing gigs, like research or strategy consulting, where I get to leverage my experience and expertise and charge by the hour. Those projects are few and far between but pay far more so it evens things out in the long run.

3. One of the biggest struggles freelancers face is setting rates. How did you approach pricing yourself in the beginning, and what advice do you have for others?

Yes, this is the hardest. I actually went by basic international rates to get a sense of what an hour of my time is worth. Then I noticed what people with a decade more of experience in their fold were charging, so now I know what's the next figure to aim for at some point in future.

4. Late payments and inconsistent work are common freelance struggles. What systems should freelancers have in place to ensure financial stability and avoid cash

crunches? Do you have any other systems that help you plan your long-term finances like retirement, health insurance etc.?

Yes, I was really concerned about late payments. So, honestly, I waited till I could get a gig that's freelance but long term and promises a steady income every month, that I use for planning long-term finances. For other projects, I'm mostly inclined towards working with international companies because the pay makes sense (when you multiply the currency) and they tend not to delay on payments.

5. Finally, while freelancing gives you the power to live your work life on your terms, do you ever feel like your corporate paycheck peers are getting ahead much quicker than you are? How do you deal with the financial FOMO that happens when you see them reaching certain milestones (maybe a nice car, or they bought their first home etc.) ahead of you? How do you find that balance in today's hyper-material social media world?

I thankfully don't have a lot of material aspirations although there is a tiny hedonist inside me. Going independent was not the first choice. I wanted to leave my previous job due to certain principles of journalism I uphold. But when I started looking out, I found I was unemployable at most places because of the salary I was earning as a mid-senior level journalist. It was appalling to know just how badly paid we all are. That is how the idea of going independent came about. So, I get some portion of what I used to make in my full-time job from a regular freelance gig and it gives me the option to make up the deficit by taking up other non-conflicting projects. Which, actually, is great overall because it allows me to finally explore different ways of monetising my experience and my reporting-writing skills.

4

An Introduction to Income Tax: What, Why, and How

I have many feelings about taxes that I can't reveal publicly. Perhaps one day when you and I meet, you can ask me this question directly. But what I will share is that understanding the tax system is an essential requirement to planning your finances efficiently. While most of us understand the basics of taxation—that you have to pay income tax when you make money over a certain limit or that it's a cut we give the government to keep essential services running—knowing how the system works can help us design our personal finances in a more elegant way, and prevent us from taking haphazard decisions.

Does Being a Taxpayer Make You Special?

When you pay income tax, you're contributing to nation building. But does it make you special? Yes and no. While paying income tax makes you a 'formal' taxpayer, the truth is that anyone who consumes—whether it's groceries, eating out, taking a taxi—is also paying tax indirectly through

GST (Goods and Services Tax). So, we're all taxpayers, in a way.

The Income Tax Act 1961 vs Income Tax Code

The Income Tax Act 1961, which currently governs how we pay our taxes in India, is 64 years old—probably why the government believed it was time to give it a facelift.

The Income Tax Code, which was introduced in 2025, is not a drastically different version of the Income Tax Act, and that wasn't the goal either. Think of it as a pre and post makeover scene from any of your favourite romantic comedies or reality shows. It's the same person, but with like, better eyebrows and nicer fitting clothes. Over the years, thousands (this is not an exaggeration) of amendments and notifications were issued, creating a maze of rules that made tax compliance a legitimate nightmare for both individuals and businesses.

The language is simpler, the calculations are easier, and tech has been introduced, but the real question is, what does this mean for you and me? What has changed, and what remains the same?

What the New Code Means for You and Me

The new tax code has not been implemented yet, and we are very much still being governed by the Income Tax Act, 1961. That said, the new code brings about a few significant changes, starting with simplified language. The code ensures that we no longer need to do mental gymnastics to understand the differences between Previous Year and

Assessment Year. There will now only be a single term: Tax Year, to represent the year for which the taxes were filed. This, and several other simpler language changes have been introduced not only for you and me to understand the law better, but also with the intention of reducing tax disputes. After all, if the law is easier to interpret, there shouldn't be differences in opinion, or at least that's the hope.

New Regime vs Old Regime

As a precursor to the code, the new tax regime was introduced within the existing Act. The new regime is simpler, easier to understand and is straightforward to calculate.

If you're filing taxes for the *first* time, know that you'll automatically fall under the new tax regime. But if you're a tax veteran who has carefully put together investments and deductions in line with the old regime, fret not, because you still get the option of choosing the old regime.

While the new income tax regime sounds simple and enticing, there are both pros and cons to it.

Pros of the New Regime

- **Lower tax rate**: The new tax regime offers a lower tax rate as compared to the old regime, which can result in higher take-home pay for taxpayers.
- **Simpler, easier to understand form:** The new tax regime is simpler and easier to understand as it does away with various deductions and exemptions, which can be complicated and time-consuming.

The income tax form you've to fill out is also more straightforward.

- **Invest how you want:** The biggest advantage of this scheme is that it allows you to invest money the way you want to, versus being coaxed into dime-a-dozen 'tax saving' schemes which may have never made sense for you in the first place. The new tax scheme gives you greater agency over your investments.
- **Brownie points**: The government is trying harder each year to push people towards the new scheme since it's far more simplified, and as a result, doesn't need the level of administration and overseeing that the old one did. And pushing people towards a certain scheme usually means that there's a lot more incentive that will be offered over the coming years for taxpayers who're opting for the new regime. Case in point: In the 2025 budget, there was a massive rate cut enabling those earning 12.75 lakh and under to pay no tax.

Cons of the New Scheme

- **Practically no deductions or opportunities for tax planning:** The new tax regime does not allow taxpayers to claim deductions, which can result in a higher tax liability for taxpayers who were availing of various deductions in the old regime. So, if you've already been taking advantage of these deductions—let's say you've invested in some long-term insurance schemes, for example, or taken a home loan—the new scheme is probably not for you.

OLD VS NEW REGIME

Feature	Old Regime	New Regime
Basic Exemption Limit	₹2.5 Lakhs	₹4 Lakhs
Income Tax Rebate Limit	₹5 Lakhs	₹12 Lakhs
Standard Deduction for Salaried Taxpayers	₹50,000	₹75,000
Beneficial For	High earners (over ₹50L) with deductions over ₹7 Lakhs	Tax payers with income under ₹50L or high earners with fewer or no deductions

So, Who Should Pick the New Income Tax Regime?

The new tax regime is built for first-time earners and young professionals. If you've just started earning, it's likely that you've not made too many 'tax saving' investments. The new regime also offers you the benefit of a lower tax rate which results in higher take-home pay.

Finally, the new regime is also very simple to understand, so if you're just starting out, this is a great way to be more confident about your taxes and take charge of your finances.

That said, if your income is on the higher end, (roughly) over ₹24 lakh, and you have tax deductions over ₹7.5 lakh, you're better off with the old regime. The benefits of the old regime are primarily for those with high tax deductions and allowances. If you don't have too many deductions in terms of, say, house rent allowance, a home loan, or education loan, or tax saver investments, you're better off with the new regime.

Remember, for as long as you *don't* have business income (which we'll talk about later in this chapter), you get the option of choosing between the old and new regime every year. Take the time to figure out which regime would be more beneficial for you for that year before you file your returns.

What the 'Income' in the Income Tax Act Stands for

When you think of income, it may seem straightforward—money coming into your bank account. But for the sake of tax, the Income Tax Act (now the Income Tax Code) categorises income into five distinct heads.

Each category has different rules for taxation, deductions, and exemptions. Understanding these classifications helps you see how the government views your earnings and, more importantly, how you can optimise your tax liability.

1. *Income from Salary*

If you are employed, your earnings fall under Income from Salary. This includes your basic salary, house rent allowance (HRA), bonuses, commissions, leave encashment, and even the value of perks like ESOPs, a company car, and so on. Your employer will pre-emptively deduct tax at source (TDS) before you receive your salary in your bank account. But remember that your employer's deduction is only an approximation, so you have to file your return to determine if you'll get a refund of extra tax deducted, or if you'll have to pay an additional amount in case enough tax wasn't deducted.

Deductions and Exemptions

- Standard deduction of ₹75,000 (as of 2025) applies to all salaried individuals under the new regime. If you're in the old regime though, your deduction is only ₹50,000.
- If you live in a rented place and you've opted for the old regime, then you get an HRA exemption that's the lowest of:
    - The HRA component of your salary
    - 50% of your basic salary (if you live in a metro, 40% for other cities), or
    - The actual rent you've paid reduced by 10% of your basic salary
- Any other exemptions as specified in the old regime.

2. *Income from House Property*

If you own a property—doesn't matter if it's commercial or residential—and earn rent from it, this falls under Income from House Property. But what if the house you own is the one you're staying in? The Income Tax Act allows you to have up to two such 'self-occupied' houses so you don't have to recognise any income coming from it.

If you have three properties but don't earn rent from any of them, you'll only be allowed the first two, and will have to recognise the third as a 'rented' property and pay tax on it.

Deductions

- Renting the property out? You'll be allowed to deduct a flat 30% of the rent you earn as a standard deduction to cover for repairs, maintenance etc.
- **New Regime:** If the property you rented out was bought on loan, you'll be allowed to reduce the interest you paid on your loan from the rent you received. In case you paid more interest than the rent you received, you can carry the loss forward for 8 years until it gets exhausted. However, you can't use this loss to reduce your other incomes, like salaries or interest. You can only set this off against future house property income or other house property incomes.
- **Old Regime:** The old regime is more beneficial to homeowners in that it allows you to extend your house property loss of up to ₹2 lakh to other heads of income. So, let's say you paid more interest than rent you received by ₹3 lakh. You can take ₹2 lakh of this loss and set it off against your other incomes. The balance ₹1 lakh gets carried forward to the next year. What's more, the old regime also allows you

to claim interest of ₹2 lakh on the house you're living in (self-occupying, in tax terms).

- In short, if you're a new homeowner and you've taken a loan, it's very likely that the old regime is more beneficial for you.

3. *Income from Capital Gains*

When you sell an asset (like stocks, real estate, or mutual funds) and make a profit, the profit you make—and not the total amount you receive—is taxed under Capital Gains. So if you buy something for ₹100 and sell it for ₹150, the tax you have to pay is calculated on the gain of ₹50.

The tax rate depends on the type of asset and the holding period:

- **If you've held an asset for less than 24 months:** For equity shares or mutual funds that are listed, you'll pay a flat 20% capital gains tax. For other assets (like land, for example), the gain will be included in your income and taxed at the same rate as your other income (also known as 'slab rate' or 'normal rate')
- **If you've held an asset for more than 24 months:** For equity shares or equity oriented mutual funds that are listed, you'll pay 12.5% on gains over and above ₹1.25 lakh. For other assets like real estate, you have two options. You can either pay a flat 12.5% on the profit, or pay 20% on the gain after 'indexation'. The indexation benefit allows you to

bring the cost of the asset to present rates, because it's not really fair to calculate a gain using a cost that pertained to many years prior. But the downside of choosing the benefit is a higher rate of tax.

- **This section needs a Chartered Accountant:** If you're thinking of buying or selling a property or any other large asset, DEFINITELY consult a CA *before* you go ahead with the transaction. They'll be able to help you plan this transaction in the most tax efficient way possible.

4. *Income from Business or Profession*

Have a hustle? Then this section is for you. Self-employed professionals, freelancers, and business owners fall under this category. This includes earnings from consulting, trading, manufacturing, or any business activity.

Deductions

- Business expenses (rent, salaries, depreciation, travel, marketing) are deductible.
- Freelancers and consultants can deduct expenses like laptops, internet, co-working spaces, and professional development costs.
- If you're an individual whose total receipts are under ₹50 lakh for the year, you can also opt for a convenient system called 'presumptive taxation'. Here, you don't need to maintain books or expenses. You get a flat 50% deduction for expenses and the remaining 50% is assumed as profit on which you

pay tax. It's very convenient and recommended for up-and-coming professionals or freelancers (unless you're spending more than 50%, in which case you might want to look both into your records and your business model).

5. *Income from Other Sources*

This is a catch-all category for earnings that do not fit into the other four heads. It includes:

- Interest from fixed deposits (FDs) and savings accounts.
- Dividends from stocks and mutual funds.
- Lottery winnings, gifts, or inheritance (subject to specific rules).
- Pension from sources other than employment.

And there you have it. The five heads of income tax. Think of it like a mythical monster. From a distance it might seem daunting, but know that every head has its own rules, deductions, and exemptions. And once you understand what each head needs, you'll be able structure your earnings efficiently, minimise taxes, and put this monster to bed without any fear of it biting you when you least expect.

The Only Deduction that Makes Sense Now: 80CCD(2)

The once venerated Chapter VI-A, dedicated purely to income tax deductions, now only exists in the old regime. In my mind, none of these deductions make sense anymore, especially if your income is below ₹40 lakh, the new regime is still friendlier for your earnings even after skipping these deductions.

By removing this chapter, the authorities have given taxpayers the ability to choose investments that are right for their financial goals, versus forcing them to put money in 'tax saving' schemes that lock money up in inefficient investments.

That said, if there's one deduction that's applicable in the new regime (and is truly tax efficient), it's the Corporate NPS scheme. In this scheme, your employer can match your NPS investment (up to 14% of your basic salary) and this contribution is tax deductible **upto ₹7.5 lakh.**

Not only does this mean a greater corpus for you (because your employer is matching your contribution), but it single-handedly saves you more taxes than any other combination of 'tax saving' investments can today.

Make Tax Deductions Work for You

Why bother knowing about tax deductions? By knowing your limits, you'll be able to avoid unnecessary 'investments' that promise to save tax, but don't really. And by staying on top of what you're eligible for, you can update your HR every year in advance. The lower the tax you've to pay, the lower that is deducted from your salary each month, and the more that you have for yourself! Now that's worth the effort.

Exemptions, Deductions, and Rebates

So we just discussed tax deductions, and you may have come across words like exemptions or rebates too in the context of income tax. If they confuse you, know that you're not alone—and not to be blamed!

Tax exemptions, deductions, and rebates all achieve the same result. They will reduce the amount of tax you pay to the authorities. But that is all that they have in common. Exemptions, deductions, and rebates otherwise work very differently.

What Exactly Are Tax Exemptions?

We pay tax on any and all incomes that we earn. An exemption refers to a specific type of income that doesn't have to be included in this calculation of total income. It is exempt. When a person's PF matures, for example, and the total amount lands up in their bank account, it is exempt from tax. So, when they calculate their total income for that year, the maturity amount or the 'exempt income' will not be a part of that calculation.

Essentially, exempt income is money that will not to be eligible for tax. This is covered under section 10 of the Income Tax Act.

All Income Received – Exempt Income = Total Income

What Are Tax Deductions?

A tax deduction, on the other hand, refers to an amount that is reduced from your total income. Continuing with the previous example, let us say this person has received their PF amount, ₹25,00,000, and also has some interest coming in from FDs, ₹3,00,000, and some contract payments of ₹5,00,000 that year. Since the amount at that lands up in their bank account when a PF matures is exempt from tax, the ₹25,00,000 is not included in their total calculation of income. Their gross total income for that year then is ₹8,00,000 (from the FDs and contract payments).

If, say, they contributed ₹1,00,000 to NPS (in total) they are eligible to deduct this amount from the total income of ₹8,00,000, resulting in a taxable income of ₹7,00,000. It is on this ₹7,00,000 that tax is calculated.

Total Income – Deductions = Taxable Income

What Are Tax Rebates?

Tax rebates are reductions on the tax you have to pay. It is not a reduction from your income, but your tax liability. And it kicks in only after you calculate it.

Today (specifically, financial year 2025-2026), if your taxable income i.e., income after deductions, is ₹12,00,000 or under (₹12,75,000 if you're salaried) you'll be eligible for a rebate under section 87A. This means that the tax you'd have otherwise had to pay, is waived off. This rebate keeps changing year on year, so it's good to stay updated on what this number is. Whatever tax you may have paid in advance (by way of TDS), will get refunded to your account.

Total Tax Payable – Rebates = Net Tax Payable

This Was a Vocabulary Lesson

If taxes were simple, the common man would have a lot more questions (and CAs would have way less work!). That said, it's important to learn these words so you can figure out what's going on in your salary sheet.

One easy way to remember these three terms is to remember the order. Exemptions come first when you calculate tax. They define the amount of money you will show as income that is eligible for tax.

Once you've defined total income, you are eligible for deductions from your total income. This will help you arrive at taxable income. The total tax you have to pay is calculated on taxable income.

And finally, rebates, if you are eligible for them, are reduced from your tax liability.

Exemptions—> Deductions—> Rebate
(Egg Dosa Roll is one way to remember it.)

Understanding and appreciating the differences between these terms not only helps build confidence when talking about the subject, but also assists in financial decision making. Nuance is power!

Why You Need to File Your Taxes

With great salaries come...great tax responsibilities. Actually, even the not-so-great salaries come with tax responsibilities. 'Filing taxes' is probably the answer to 'What is the opposite of sexy?', but it's one of the most important financial habits to cultivate early in your career.

Your ITR Is the Pudding

Many first-time earners tend to deprioritise or sometimes ignore filing their taxes altogether. After all, why file if you don't even earn enough to pay tax, right? Wrong! Even if your income is below the taxable threshold (currently ₹4LPA for most taxpayers), filing an Income Tax Return (ITR) shows discipline on your part, and is considered to be your financial resume, in a way.

You need ITRs when you apply for loans, visas, or even freelance work with some big clients. I needed to share my ITRs for writing this book! Banks and financial institutions look at your ITRs as evidence that you're financially stable. Filing consistently builds a positive credit profile, opens doors to better loan terms, and signals to countries across the world that you're a legitimate, disciplined citizen who respects the law.

Not Filing Can Be Expensive

The deadline for filing your ITR usually falls on 31 July (unless the government extends it). Missing this date can lead to penalties of up to ₹5,000. So unnecessary.

Good Refunds Come to Those Who File

Remember the TDS (Tax Deducted at Source) your employer deducts from your paycheck? Or that extra deduction from your freelance gig payments? Filing your ITR is the only way to claim that money back if you've paid more tax than you owe.

After all, what's worse than paying extra tax? Not getting back the money that's rightfully yours!

It's the Law

Listen, your PAN and AADHAR card are more or less linked to every transaction you make these days. And while the IT Department isn't watching you (or so they say), skipping on filing your ITR could get you flagged—especially if you've had large transactions (like a freelance windfall or capital gains). Filing on time ensures you stay on the right side of the law, no questions asked.

HOW TO MAKE FILING YOUR ITR LESS SCARY, INTIMIDATING, AND/OR ANNOYING

- **Mark the date:** Set a reminder in your calendar for June, so you have enough time to gather your documents.
- **Use online platforms:** Filing has become super simple, thanks to new-age fintech platforms like ClearTax. The forms on the Income Tax website are also a lot simpler than they used to be.
- **Get help if you need it:** If your finances are even a little complicated (like extra freelance income), consult a CA—it's worth the fee.

An Introduction to Income Tax—The TL; DR

Why Do We Even Pay Taxes?

Simply put, income tax is the government's way of keeping the country running. If you earn above a certain threshold, you're expected to contribute your fair share—just like how everyone chips in for a dinner bill (except, you know, with actual consequences if you don't).

You're Already a Taxpayer (Even If You Think You Aren't!)

Even if you've never filed an income tax return, you're still paying tax—every time you buy something, eat out, or book a cab, GST is already baked into the price. So, surprise! You've been funding the economy all along.

Old vs. New Tax Regime: What's the Deal?

India's new tax code is designed to be easier to understand and offers lower tax rates, but with fewer deductions. If you're a first-time earner or not big on tax-saving investments, the new regime might be better for you. But if you've carefully planned your finances around deductions (hello, home-loan folks), the old regime might still be worth sticking to.

Deductions, Exemptions, and Rebates— What's the Difference?

- Exemptions: Certain types of income (like EPF maturity amounts) don't count as taxable income at all.
- Deductions: You can subtract specific expenses (like insurance premiums, tuition fees, and home loan interest) from your taxable income, reducing how much tax you owe.
- Rebates: Even after all that, if your taxable income is below ₹12 lakh (under the new regime), you get an extra rebate, meaning your tax liability could be zero.

Why Filing Your Taxes Is a Power Move

Even if you're not required to file a return (because your income is below the taxable limit), doing so can unlock a ton of benefits—like getting tax refunds, building your financial credibility, and avoiding unnecessary penalties. Plus, if you ever need a visa, loan, or credit card upgrade, your ITR is like your financial résumé.

The One Deduction You Should Still Care About

In the new regime, most deductions are gone—but the Corporate NPS (80CCD(2)) is still a winner. If your employer contributes to your NPS account, it's tax-free up to ₹7.5 lakh per year.

Final Takeaway: Taxes Don't Have to Be a Headache

Instead of scrambling at the last minute (or ignoring taxes altogether), get familiar with the basics. Know which tax regime works best for you, understand the deductions you qualify for, and file your returns on time. The more you know, the less you'll overpay—and the more of your hard-earned money stays with you.

5

Go Forth and Invest

What Costing Taught Me about Investing

When I was studying for my Chartered Accountancy exams, the intermediate exams to be specific, I had enrolled in cost accounting classes that were taught by one Mr B. Now, while every paper in this exam was considered to be hard to pass, cost accounting or costing as it was fondly referred to, was the Kraken. It was as feared as it was detested for it required students to process long, convoluted questions that required detailed calculations within an impossible 3-hour time limit.

Mr B had a cult following among many students and it was easy to see why. He was savvy, articulate, and smooth. He'd regale his students with stories of his own experiences, mixing in industry gossip and investing wisdom for good measure. He'd explore concepts that didn't pertain to the syllabus and insisted that if we were to succeed, we had to broaden our views of the world and look at the bigger picture. He'd give his students the confidence that costing was not a subject to be feared if one understood what lay at its core.

I went into the exams with this conviction, that my CoNcEpTuAl UnDeRsTaNdInG and fearlessness, coupled with my reading of the syllabus in full, would ensure a passing grade.

I got 19 out of 100 in that paper. What was more devastating was the fact that had I gotten the bare minimum of 40 marks, I would have cleared both groups—and consequently the CA intermediate level—in full.

For my second attempt, I went to Mr P. He was not known for his conceptual explorations or his stories. He was old school. If Mr B was the master at handwaving, Mr P was the master at…handwriting. He would tirelessly write formula after formula on his board for every chapter while ensuring that we wrote as much as he did, if not more. You learned the formula. You applied the formula. You learned the framework. You applied the framework. Your mind and hands had no time or space to even consider the existence of a bigger picture. 'Your job,' he would tell us, 'is not to understand concepts. It is to pass the exam. You will have time to enjoy the concept at leisure, after you pass.'

I hated the classes, although I stuck to them because the fees had already been paid. But after the first week, I realised that the constant practice coupled with set frameworks made me better at articulating solutions and faster at solving problems. The more I did, the more I understood and the more I understood, the more I realised how less I knew. Mr P taught us the importance of knowing the basic concepts in-depth vs everything at a superficial level.

When I sat down for my exams the second time, I wrote them with the confidence of someone who'd solved 500 plus problems during the course of the previous month. I knew I wouldn't have all the answers but that my brain and my fingers could work together to spot patterns, uncover the concept and apply the necessary framework to solve them.

I got 67 out of 100.

The reason I indulged in this lengthy story, dear reader, is because investing is very similar. It's very easy to get swayed by the endless gyaan and handwaving on investing that is so freely available all around us. Instead of being overwhelmed or carried away by what you read about mutual funds, stocks, gold, cryptocurrency, NFTs, and everything else that's out there, ask yourself: Will this help me pass my exam?

Here, the exam is your life. Your goals. Your dreams, your shortcomings, your ambitions, your obligations. It is your retirement, your master's degree, your vacation home, the education you want to give your child, the emergencies you want to be prepared for. With the right selection of investments, you can pass your exam with flying colours.

Define Your Goals

The idea of investing is alluring, but often times, the effort involved in getting started is enough to put one off the exercise altogether. But this can be tackled if we break this down into smaller components, starting with the 'why'. Our 'why's are our North Star. They ensure that we don't get lost or overwhelmed. Our 'why's are also very unique to us, our lives, our dreams, and more crucially, our circumstances. So don't ever compare your 'why' to someone else's.

Plan SMART

'I need to be rich' is not a goal. Neither is 'I need to retire.' SMART (Specific, Measurable, Achievable, Relevant, and Time-bound) goals are ideal, but the process of putting together a SMART goal can also be overwhelming since there are so many parameters.

That said, if you have a process, it becomes easier, so here's mine. If my goal is to travel more, for example, I start with getting *specific*.

- ⇨ Where do I want to go?
- ⇨ When do I want to go?
- ⇨ Who do I want to go with?
- ⇨ How long will this trip be?

The answers to these questions will form the first part of your goal. Let's say I want to go to Spain, next year, with my family, and for a week. Now that I've gotten the specifics, I need to move on to *measurability.*

This is the (un-fun) part where I find out how much it's going to cost me and how much I need to save for this particular trip. Tickets to Spain from Chennai for three of us come at around ₹1.5 lakh for the dates we're looking at (you can use a tool like SkyScanner to get the best prices). We prefer Airbnbs as a family (you get more space and a kitchen) and the one we like comes to around ₹70,000 in total. Add in another ₹70,000 for eating out and tickets to experiences etc, it all works out to ₹3 lakh. Family travel means adding a 10-20% buffer, just in case.

So now I know I'll have to save ₹3,60,000 for a family holiday to Spain. But how long do I have to do this?

That's when you look at *time.* Assuming I want to go to Spain next summer, I can give myself 8 months or I can give myself 12 months. Let's make it 12 months. That would mean I need to save ₹30,000 a month for a year.

Now I ask myself, is this *achievable?* Looking at my household's income, our existing expenses and investments, ₹30,000 is doable (for me). But what if it's not doable for you? That's when you start to adjust. You can either give yourself more time (₹15,000 over two years), or maybe cut down on existing discretionary expenses—fewer extended nights out, perhaps—to make it work. This is the part where you're honest to yourself about making it work.

Now put it all together: My goal is to **travel to Spain next year with my family**, for which I'll need to save **₹30,000 every month for 12 months**. Now this is a SMART goal.

Here's another with a slightly longer term view. Let's say you want to save for your child's higher education. You'll start by getting specific.

- What am I saving for? Their under-graduation or their masters?
- How many years do I have before they get there?
- Where will they study? In India or abroad?
- What are they interested in? What is their line of study likely to be?

Once you have your answers, you want to measure. How much will their education cost? Will you be able to save in full? Or is the plan to help them with a solid part-payment? Fees for nearly every university in the world these days is public information.

Let's assume I want to save ₹50,00,000 for my child's higher education in the next 10 years. On the face of it, it can seem intimidating to say 'I need to save five lakhs a year.' But the advantages you have with long term goals are that:

1. You can step up your savings as you earn more with career growth. So even if you can only save a lakh a year for your child's education today, you can increase it to 2 lakh next year.
2. Compounding is more effective in the long term. So even the smaller savings you make towards your goal will multiply into a significant number over time.

So if I put it together, it will be: I will save for my child's education by investing ₹15,000 every month for 10 years, with 20% annual increments.

Take Time for Goal Setting

If there's one thing I want you to take away from this chapter, it's that good goals take time and research. You really need to spend some time to think about exactly what you want—is it a holiday? Or is it to keep up with your friends' Instagram feeds? The more time you spend thinking about *what* you want, the clearer you'll be about how you'll get there, and sometimes, whether you want to get there at all.

WHAT'S THE MAXIMUM YOU CAN SPEND ON 'WANTS'?

Common wisdom around saving for discreet experiences like travel, or any kind of splurge for that matter, is to not cross 10% of your combined household income net of EMIs.

That's 10% x (Combined annual income—EMIs). If your household income is ₹60 lakh and you pay ₹20 lakh in EMIs, your travel budget will be ₹4 lakh (10% x (60–20)).

Remember, when saving for experiences, especially if it's with family, you might want to rethink the way you balance cost and convenience. Plan for the trip you *want* to take.

If you focus on getting the cheapest prices—especially for experiences like travel—one of two things will happen: you'll either stick to your budget and be miserable, or you'll spiral way out of budget and be miserable. By being realistic about the kind of holiday you want to have, the experiences you want to attend and the places you want to eat in, you'll be able to estimate your experiences much more accurately and have a comfortable budget—even if that means waiting longer.

The Long, Medium, and Short of It

The more you articulate your wants, you'll see that your goals will be of varying timelines. A holiday in the next year, your child's higher education fund in 10 years, a down payment for a home in the next 5 years, or putting together an emergency fund in the next 6 months. You'll also find yourself dealing with *multiple* goals within the same timeline.

So how do you pick what to chase?

Here's an approach that has worked for me—stick to 1 or 2 goals in the short-and-medium term (up to 5 years), and up to 3 in the long term (more than 5 years). The ability to strike off short-term goals goes a long way in building financial confidence (not to mention, it is *incredibly satisfying*). But too many short-term goals will find you getting frustrated at not being able to achieve them. Having multiple long-term goals (up to 3, ideally), on the other hand, allows you take advantage of the compounding effect, where even small amounts of money can snowball over time. It gives you a foundation to build on as your income levels increase over time.

So set yourself up for success by focusing on 1-2 short-and-medium-term goals and up to 3 long-term goals.

Why You Need to Know What Your Risk Profile Is

Okay, so you know what to save for. But before you jump into investing, you need to know your risk profile.

Your risk profile represents the amount of risk you're willing to take as an investor. And your ability to absorb risks will determine how much money you'll be able to make in the markets. When it comes to investing, risk isn't a bad thing. In fact, it's necessary. But the amount of finance (mis)information out there on the internet today means that there are thousands of young investors who're actively losing money in the name of 'risk taking'.

The Indian stock markets are governed by the Securities Exchange Board of India (SEBI). They're the 'watchdog', who make sure that no foul play occurs in the markets. SEBI was instituted in the aftermath of the Harshad Mehta scam (if you've not watched *Scam 1992*, I'd highly recommend it!) and every year, they share data to help the public understand the markets better.

In 2024, they reported a number of startling findings around Futures & Options trading, a highly technical and complicated method of making (or losing) money in the markets. For starters, 43% of F&O traders were under the age of 30. What's more, 93% of individual traders made losses in 2024 with the average loss clocking at ₹2,00,000.[1] SEBI has openly called out finance influencers on various channels who peddle 'advice' to be the root cause of this alarming situation. SEBI has also banned influencers and put down rules (for example, you have to be 'qualified' now to give finance advice), but it all feels like too little too late.

The stock market has become a casino.

This isn't an 'Indian' problem either. In the United States, there are now 'Gamblers Anonymous' communities, modelled after Alcoholics Anonymous, to help young people recognise and recover from their addiction to risky stock market trades. The adrenaline rush—and the *crack cocaine* nature of risky trading—is akin to riding a roller coaster without safety belts on: Injuries are guaranteed.

And that's why risk needs to be calculated and tailored to your life, your personality, and your circumstances. Knowing your risk profile will inform your investment choices and ensure you stay away from anything that can cripple your finances.

What Kind of Risk Taker Are You?

Broadly, there are about 5 categories of risk takers:

1. **The Safety First Investor**: The conservative investor for whom safety/retrieval of funds is paramount. They're okay with making minimal returns in return for minimal or no risk. A safety first investor is happy making ₹5 on his investment of ₹100, if it means that he won't lose anything.

2. **The Training Wheels Investor**: The moderately conservative investor who is willing to take small risks in exchange for proportionate returns in the long term. The training wheels investor would try to make ₹8 on his investment of ₹100, but would also be okay if it means that he might lose ₹2 trying to do so.

3. **The Speed and Seatbelt Investor:** The moderately aggressive investor who is willing to take moderate risks for slightly increased returns in the medium and long term. The speed and seatbelt investor is comfortable losing up to ₹5 in the short term if it means that he'll make ₹15 on his investment of ₹100 in the medium to short term.

4. The Calculated Risk Taker: The aggressive investor who is willing to take significant risks in exchange for high returns over the long term. The calculated risk taker is okay with his portfolio moving around, sometimes losing up to ₹15 on his investment if it means he'll make anywhere between ₹30-35 on his investment of ₹100 over the long term.

5. The Adrenaline Junkie: The very aggressive investor who is willing to take high levels of risk in the long and short term for maximum returns. The adrenaline junkie would look to make ₹70-100 (double) on their investment of ₹100, but they're taking on this bet knowing that they could potentially lose ₹50-70 on their investment.

What Should Your Risk Profile Be?

General investing wisdom states that the younger you are, the more risk you can take because risk wears down in the long term. And by long term, we're talking 15-20 years, minimum. Warren Buffet, for reference, evened his risks out over a period of 50 years. So if you're in your early 20s, you can afford to start out with the riskier investment classes like equities, which we'll be talking about further in this chapter.

But what you should know is that risk profiles are a spectrum, not a point. All of us fall in different places on that spectrum. Your risk profile isn't just based on your age, it's also based on your personal ability to roll with the dips as well as your financial circumstances.

You could be young, but your parents and siblings

depend on you, so you're risk averse. Maybe you saw your parent or an elder lose money in the markets, which put you off it. You could be in your late 40s, but with enough savings or a large enough income that can allow you to take risks.

An important but never-talked-about aspect of investing is that money is emotional and we're not formulae. You can't substitute the letters with numbers and expect the same result each time. We are products of our lived experiences and extending rules like '100 minus your age is the percentage of risky assets your portfolio can contain' is reductive and manufactures anxiety in the place of confidence.

There is no 'right' risk profile, the same way there is no 'right' way to invest. It's simply your way.

4 Questions to Ask Yourself Before You Invest in ANYTHING

What Is It?

Ask yourself: Is it truly an asset? What am I putting my money in? Can I explain what I've invested in to my 8 year old niece or nephew?

Why Does this Exist?

What purpose does it serve? This is slightly philosophical, but ask yourself: Am I putting money in something that is creating wealth or am I just showing status? Think about it this way: Shares in BMW will create wealth in the future. Buying an actual BMW on the other hand, will show status, but what you have on hand is ultimately a car that depreciates in value.

Why Am I Considering This?

Am I doing it because of independent thought or is it because of herd mentality? Do I trust my decision because I did my research or am I riding on my friend's confidence? If you build conviction then you are fundamentally sound. If you borrow conviction, then you're just playing poker with someone else's hand.

Who Are the People Behind This?

It's vital to know the motivations behind the people who're running the show. Are you catering to your interests? Or theirs? Your investments must only have your interests at heart.

Why Building Your Portfolio Is Like Making Garam Masala

There's a reason why there's no single recipe or source for garam masala—because every single household has different preferences for how they like their curries. While the basic spice blend is homogenous, the proportions of the spices are changed to suit tastes.

Creating a portfolio is not very different from making your own garam masala. A good portfolio is tailored to your tastes, appetite (risk), and preferences. Putting it together is not complex (since the ingredients are standard), but arriving at the best blend for you requires thought.

Good masalas are made of high-quality spices. A well-balanced portfolio, is made of high quality investments, like:

1. Stocks and Shares/Mutual Funds
2. Fixed Deposits/Recurring Deposits
3. Gold
4. Provident Fund/National Pension Scheme
5. Insurance
6. Real Estate
7. Art and Collectibles

Your job is to arrive at a selection or mix of investments that is capable of both providing growth as well as mitigating risks.

Once you understand the role of each investment in helping you achieve your goals, you'll be able to arrive at the right mix.

PAUSE A MINUTE

Dearest reader, this is the longest chapter in the book. It's a novella by itself and will likely overwhelm you if you're encountering all of this for the first time. So what I ask you to do is this: pick a single asset class, like mutual funds, or stocks, or real estate. Read about it, and move on to the following chapters. When you're ready to learn something new, come back. This chapter—and all its wisdom—will stay here, waiting for you.

Understanding Debt and Equity

If you're new to investing, you'll see the words debt and equity being thrown around everywhere. But what is debt? And what is equity?

We have to start with understanding how companies work.

Every business starts with money. This is called capital—basically, the cash you need to make things happen. When a business is registered under The Companies Act, it becomes a company. And this is where things get interesting: the capital is broken down into tiny units called shares.

Imagine you're starting a company with ₹1,00,000. You decide to split this money into 10,000 shares worth ₹10 each. That ₹10 is called the face value of the share.

The whole ₹1,00,000? That's your company's *equity*—which is just another word for ownership. The math is simple: whoever owns the most shares owns the biggest chunk of the company.

But here's the thing about running a company: as it grows, it needs more money—the kind that the founders might not really have. At this point, companies have two options:

1. *Borrow from financial institutions or go into debt*

When companies borrow from financial institutions, they need to pay interest on their loans, just like us. And this interest needs to be paid out, irrespective of whether they're making a profit or a loss. On the flip side, the investment cannot grow beyond the interest that the company is paying.

So when you're putting money in a debt investment, it's not very different from lending money. You'll get an assured—but restricted—return.

2. *Raise more capital or equity*

When a company goes public, it's giving the world a piece of the action. They can sell shares to people like you and me, and in return, they get extra cash to grow.

Now, when you buy a share, you're not just buying a random piece of paper (or, you know, a number on an app). You're buying a literal piece of the company. But don't expect to pay the ₹10 face value we talked about earlier. The price you'll pay depends on a bunch of things: How well the company is doing, what it owns, and how much people want its shares. So if the company is doing well, the market value of its shares will be way higher than the face value—when it comes to equity, the sky's the limit for growth!

But that brings us to the flip side: If the company isn't doing well, share prices can also go underground. And that's the risk when it comes to equity. After all, it isn't just bad management that can affect the company's performance. It can also be environmental factors (maybe the rains made cotton more expensive for textile giants), political factors (maybe their factory wasn't given permission to set up), and general international factors (like war) that can drive a company to ruin.

That's why we call equity risky investments, because when you buy a share, you're betting on that company's future. If it grows, you win. If it flops, you lose.

How the Stock Market Works

Picture your neighbourhood vegetable market. It's buzzing, full of vendors selling fresh produce brought in from all over—sometimes even from other countries. The stock market? It's basically the same thing, except instead of tomatoes and bhindi, you're buying a piece of companies across industries like tech, energy, and steel.

In India, we have two big stock markets: the National Stock Exchange (NSE) and the Bombay Stock Exchange (BSE). Think of these as the most popular 'markets' in town. Every company listed on these exchanges gets its performance tracked daily.

If a company is thriving and the economy is in its favour, its share price climbs. If not, they drop.

The Plural of Index Is Indices

Let's talk about indices. If listed companies were songs, then indices are the 'best of' playlists. An index is basically a way to group companies together and track how they're doing.

For example, the BSE SENSEX and the NSE NIFTY are the biggest and most important indices in India. They're called Benchmark Indices because they give us a snapshot of how the market, and by extension the economy, is doing overall.

Index vs Market

There's the market. Then why do we need an index? We need indices because there are tens of thousands 'listed companies' in India.

Indices help investors figure out whether the market is having a good day or a bad one. Sometimes, you don't need to read the story to understand what's happening. You just need to read the headlines. The stock market (or sector, like banking or IT) is the story. The index is the headline.

How Do Companies Make It into an Index?

In December 2024, Zomato, the foodtech giant, replaced JSW Steel in the SENSEX as part of the index's half-yearly 'rebalancing' exercise, where they shuffle companies to provide a more accurate picture of the overall market.

Naturally, this was *big* news. Why? Because being a part of an index like the NIFTY or SENSEX is like officially being a part of the Big Boys' Club. Not every company can be a part of the NIFTY or SENSEX shuffle. They have to:

- ⇨ Be large (think Reliance, Infosys—companies worth thousands of crores).
- ⇨ Be liquid, meaning lots of people are buying and selling their shares regularly.
- ⇨ Represent their sector well and have a solid financial track record.

So getting into an index is a pretty big deal. You're representing an entire market, after all.

Up and Down

Most indices are weighted by market capitalisation. That means that bigger companies (think Reliance or TCS) have a bigger impact on the index than smaller ones. So if a company like Reliance has a bad day, you'll see the index drop. But if it's crushing it? The index gets a nice boost.

The index's movement is generally representative of the larger sentiment in the market. The shares of the company you hold could have nothing to do with the one that's bringing the market down, but it could still fall since the overall sentiment is negative. The opposite can also be true. Your shares could still be up even if the indices are down.

How Many Indices Are There?

Apart from the SENSEX and NIFTY, we have indices for multiple reasons and seasons:

- ⇨ Sectoral Indices: Like BANKNifty or Nifty IT, which focus on banks and tech companies.
- ⇨ Thematic Indices: Think of these as niche playlists, like ESG indices for companies focused on sustainability.
- ⇨ Size-based Indices: There are mid-cap and small cap indices based on companies' sizes.

Forget the Birds and the Bees, it's the Bulls and the Bears

If the market is doing well and the index is going up, the market is called 'bullish'. Why? Because when bulls charge, they toss things up with their horns. Bears, on the other hand, throw or pin their prey to the ground. So when the market is falling, it's 'bearish'.

You Can Invest in the Index

Indices are more than just a way to keep score. These days, you can even invest directly in them through index funds or ETFs, which mirror the performance of the index. They're great if you want to invest without stressing about picking individual stocks.

The stock market really isn't so different from your vegetable market. It's just got bigger stakes—and no tomatoes.

Will You Bet on Debt?

The debt market is a lot like the introverted sibling of the stock market—not as flashy, but just as important. Debt investments might not make headlines, but they play a massive role in the financial ecosystem.

Think about it this way—if equity markets are the engines that power the economy, debt is the lubricant that ensures these big engines don't break down.

Debt is crucial for businesses. It helps them manage day-to-day operations, fund working capital, or invest in essential projects. Without debt, the economic machine might seize! And just as too much or too little lubricant can harm an engine, excessive or poorly managed debt can lead to economic instability.

That said, let me put a disclaimer upfront: The debt market is largely the playground of institutional investors, namely, banks, mutual funds, insurance companies, and the like. Individual investors like you and me will be a smaller piece of the pie. And while we will have options to invest in debt *through* these institutions, investing in the debt market directly is slightly more advanced territory.

Let's Talk about Your Options

Debt instruments are financial tools that let companies, banks, and governments borrow money. So while you become a part owner of the business when you buy stocks, here you become a part lender.

The main types of debt instruments in India include:

Government Bonds (G-Secs)

Lending money to the Government of India—sounds fancy, right? These bonds are super safe because, well, it's the government. They *have* to repay you. So the security aspect is automatically taken care of.

But here's a caveat: Most government bond investors are institutions. However, individuals like you and me can invest in these bonds thanks to the RBI finally opening its doors to us through platforms like RBI Retail Direct.

Corporate Bonds

These are like government bonds, but you're lending to a company instead. Riskier, sure, but the returns are higher.

Who's it for? Investors who are willing to take a bet on a company's credit rating and take on a bit more risk. Institutions dominate this space, but savvy individual investors can participate through brokers or mutual funds. Debt mutual funds usually invest in a bouquet of bonds, making sure this risk aspect is also diversified.

Fixed Deposits (FDs)

Yes, the humble FD, which is apparently the most hated 'investment' according to the internet. Let me tell you that they deserve a lot more love! This is where most individual investors begin their debt journey. It's simple, predictable, and familiar.

If you want a safe, straightforward option, you can't go wrong with FDs. That said, FD returns *almost never* beat inflation, so they're better for short-term goals and for keeping your emergency fund.

Corporate Fixed Deposits

These are like FDs but issued by companies instead of banks. They often come with better interest rates—but just like corporate bonds, more risk too.

Remember, credit ratings matter here. A high return could mean higher risk, so choose carefully. What's more, corporate fixed deposits also involve a few additional rounds of paperwork for you to receive your money back, so keep in mind that it's not the most convenient option either.

Debentures and T-Bills

Debentures and T-Bills are more advanced debt instruments for experienced investors who can handle a greater load of risk in the long and short terms. I wouldn't recommend them, simply because of the complexity involved in procuring them and because they're traditionally institutional investments. Sometimes, it's best to stay in our lanes as retail investors!

How Much Debt, How Much Equity?

Understanding personal finance is understanding that there's no right answer for *everyone*. Debt is great if you're saving for something near term. FDs get a bad rep on the internet these days, but in my opinion, it's still a decent option to park funds that you want to use in a year or two. Debt-focused instruments are also a good option for senior citizens who just need stable growth year on year.

Equity more or less goes up in the long run, provided you've picked the right companies and sectors that are poised for growth. Picking these shares takes time, research, and expertise...and that's where mutual funds come in.

How Mutual Funds Work

A mutual fund is a trust which pools the savings of a number of investors who share a common financial goal. The trust collects money from these investors, and the consolidated amount is invested in different types of securities by 'fund managers'.

Let's say you have four friends—Michelle, Madhavi, Kamala, and Raji. All five of you are working women, and earn a decent income. However, your savings plans are restricted to simply not spending. Now Raji's aunt and uncle have a successful share trading business, and they make great money. The idea of investing in the stock market is something that has appealed to all of you, but who has the time and energy to follow the markets all day? One day, Raji comes up with a plan. She asks you all to give a portion of your savings to her, and she will, in turn, consolidate these savings into one big amount and give the total amount to her aunt and uncle, who will invest in the stock market on her behalf. Raji will then distribute the profits based on the proportion of everyone's contribution to the total pool.

Raji is the mutual fund with whom you've entrusted the money, Raji's aunt and uncle are the fund managers who invest the money so collected, and the rest of you, are the unit holders/investors.

The type of securities that these 'fund managers' choose depends on the scheme and risk category of the mutual fund.

Why Should I Give My Money to Someone's Aunt?

Mutual funds are a smart option to save for the future. This is because they don't require a heavy initial investment, which means you can start saving slowly, and in small amounts. You can increase the amount of savings as you go, but the low investment means that they're the perfect savings tool for young and old alike.

Another reason why I'm a fan of mutual funds is because they will give you the expertise that you don't have. Fund managers, who make these investments, are professionals whose jobs are solely dedicated to following the markets and making the best decisions for their funds. That isn't to say that every fund manager is a magical money unicorn, but rest assured that mutual funds do take away the guesswork and agony that comes with investing directly.

Finally, mutual funds are transparent because they're regulated by the AMFI or Association of Mutual Funds of India and the SEBI. All information about where the mutual fund's investing in, its performance over the years, and who its fund managers are, are only a quick Google search away.

Why Mutual Funds Are the Perfect 'First' Investment

In my view—and this is a strong one—mutual funds ought to be the first investment that you make. Given the evolution of fintech in India, you can set up the investments on your phone. They're simple to understand and have so many variants—you can create a diversified portfolio with just mutual funds!

Ok, I Have 1 Lakh, Now Tell Me How This Works

Every mutual fund issues a certain number of 'units' that investors can purchase. The price per unit of a mutual fund is known as the NAV, or Net Asset Value. If you're already holding units in a mutual fund, the NAV is what you'll receive, per unit, if you were to sell it.

There are different types of plans that give you this return in different ways.

In a **Growth Plan**, the returns earned by the fund are retained in the fund, so your marker for returns is the increase in NAV.

Let's assume that the mutual fund you're interested in has an NAV of ₹250. With ₹1,00,000, you can purchase 400 units. You hold the units for one year. At the end of one year, the NAV of the fund is declared to be ₹350, which means your investment is now worth ₹1,40,000 (400 units at ₹350 per unit), giving you a return of ₹40,000 on ₹1,00,000.

If it's a **Dividend Payout Plan**, the fund will pay you back the increase in NAV by declaring dividends from time to time. Dividend plans are suited for those looking for an income, and growth plans are for those looking for a long-term investment.

There are also **Dividend Reinvestment Plans** (where the dividend declared is used to purchase more units in the fund) and **Bonus Plans** (where additional units in the fund are allotted, instead of dividend).

SIP for Success

It's not easy—or sustainable—for any of us to make large investments in a single go. And that's where mutual fund SIPs—or, Systematic Investment Plans—kick in. Here, you invest a fixed sum every month, a sum that is based on your income, and your ability to save.

The bare minimum investment for an SIP plan in most mutual funds is as low as ₹500, and you can automate these payments with bank mandates, so you neither have the hassle of remembering to make the payments, nor the excuse to miss them.

The great thing about SIPs is that you catch both the highs and the lows of the mutual fund. Let's assume that the NAV of the fund today is ₹100, and the next month, the markets do excellently. The NAV of the fund would increase, and consequently you'd get fewer units than you did the previous month. If, the month after, the markets fall, the NAV would, too, and you would get more units in the bargain for the same amount invested. So, if the market does well again, so does your profit, for you would have had extra units from the previous month's purchase.

Direct vs Regular: Is There a Difference?

If you've ever searched for a mutual fund, you'd have seen that there are two variants to the same fund: Direct and regular. There is really only one key difference between the two: Direct mutual funds are commission free, which means that no one is being paid to make you invest in them. Regular, on the other hand, will involve a commission amount that will be paid out to whoever you're investing with.

While there is no difference in *what* the mutual fund invests in, direct mutual funds will be marginally more cost effective for you, the investor. Think of it this way—the mutual fund house is spending less money to sell you this mutual fund because there are no commissions that are being paid out. And the mutual fund passes this saving on to you.

If you invest through a mutual fund advisor, it's likely that you'll be putting money in a regular mutual fund. If you're making your own mutual fund decisions, you'd have to choose a direct mutual fund.

There Are 2500 Mutual Fund Schemes Out There. Which One Do I Choose?

India's mutual fund industry has been on a roll over the last couple of years. According the to AMFI, the total Assets Under Management (AUM, or more simply, the money that's being managed) by mutual fund companies, hit 58.6 trillion rupees (around $701.90 billion) in May 2024. This marks a jump of 10 trillion rupees in under a year!

Clearly, those *Mutual Funds Sahi Hai* campaigns have worked.

But this surge in investor interest also means that fund houses have been cranking out new schemes every month, with 100+ New Fund Offerings launching in 2024 alone. Rest assured, there's plenty of mutual fund fish in the sea.

But How Does One Choose?

Start With Your Goals

Your savings goal is your starting point. Think of each goal as a bucket that needs to be filled, and the more specific you are with defining this, the better. Is it a lumpsum you'd want in 15 years for your child's education? Is it a sum you'd want as a downpayment for your dream home in about 10 years? Or is it to help fund your wedding in about 5 years? Define the purpose of the investment and how far away it is in the future.

The Farther, the Riskier

Now you have to choose the type of fund you have to invest in. Mutual funds come in many shapes, forms, and volatilities. If your goal is in the short term (the next year or so), you're better off investing in a safer instrument with a guaranteed rate of return, like an FD. If you're not a risk taker, then debt-centric funds with predictable rates of return might be the right option.

But if your goal is in the medium-to-long-term future, you can afford to take a riskier bet since the risks iron themselves out in the long term. Take a look at the graphs below. The first one shows SENSEX's movement (representative of the stock market, broadly) in a month, a year, 5 years, and since its inception in the 80s.

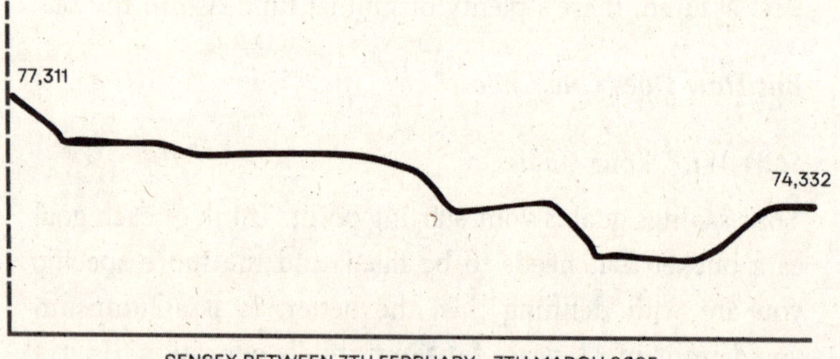

The SENSEX's movement over a month

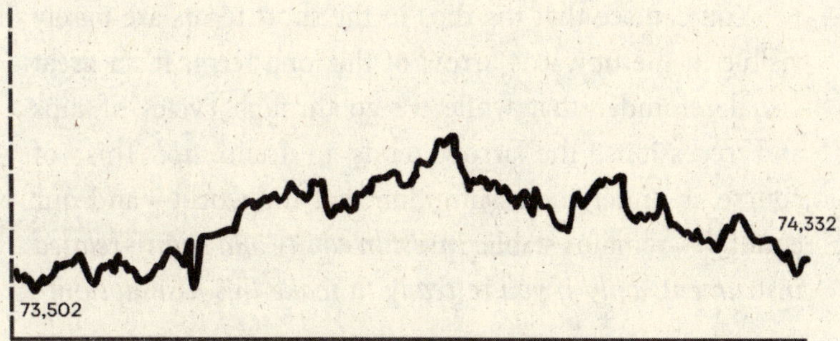

The SENSEX's movement over a year.

Below: The SENSEX's movement over the last 5 years

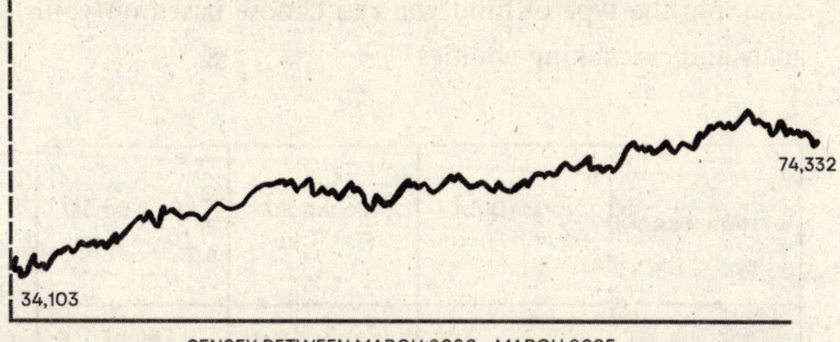

The SENSEX Since its Inception

You can see that the dips in the short terms are barely visible in the upwards arrow of the long term. It's a great visual reminder that while we go through cycles of dips and recessions, the arrow tends to trend up. This, of course, is under the assumption that the world—and our country—remains stable. *Invest in equity and equity-related instruments only if you're ready to make this assumption!*

Pick Your Fighter

Now that you know your goal and how far away it is, you can pick a fund. Here's a rough guide that can help you zone into the type of fund you can choose based on your goals and risk-taking abilities.

High Risk	Hybrid (Debt + Equity) Funds	Multi Allocation/ Flexi Cap Funds	Mid & Small Cap Funds
Medium Risk	Short Duration Debt Funds	Hybrid (Debt + Equity) Funds	Multi Allocation/ Flexi Cap Funds
Low Risk	Liquid Funds	Gold/Gilt Funds	Large Cap/Index Funds
Time Vs Risk	**Short Term (0 - 3 Years)**	**Medium Term (3 - 5 Years)**	**Long Term (5 - 10+ Years)**

Use the Internet!

Very underrated. Let's say you know you need to invest in a Flexi Cap fund. Which fund do you choose? Every noteworthy business publication has a very well researched 'top' mutual fund list—in a way they've more or less done the work for you. I personally keep track of the *Livemint 20* and the *MoneyControl 30*.

These lists have culled down the 2000+ funds out there into handy categories based on what you want to invest in, and have identified the best performers based on returns, how long the fund has been operating, the total money it manages etc.

You could get hold of an investment advisor if your ask is slightly more complex or if you want to invest a larger sum of money, but if you're just getting started, these lists make your life very easy.

Just, Start.

If you're a beginner my advice is to go one fund at a time. SIPs, which are small monthly payments are the best way to build a savings habit with mutual funds. You can start with as little as ₹500/month and keep building on top of that.

Do mutual funds/index funds beat inflation?

A reader had sent in this question, asking if mutual funds—specifically, index funds—could beat inflation. The answer is yes. Index funds on average have been returning well over 12% year on year, over the last decade. Inflation has hovered at around 5-6%.

So, to reiterate: Don't think too much! Getting started is the best way to get started.

All That Glitters—Evaluating Gold as an Investment

Growing up, I often watched my mother save whatever cash she had on hand in a special purse. Every month, she'd use this money to pay a monthly 'chit' at her favourite jeweller's. Once she'd paid 11 months' worth of instalments, she'd be eligible to buy jewellery for 12 months' value (or more). I saw my mother do this religiously over the years, and she did it not because she loved jewellery—yes, she liked the odd necklace—but because she truly believed in gold as an investment. Her logic was simple: the value of gold would never fall, and it would, therefore, always be a safe investment.

But is this true?

All That Glitters

Gold has shaped civilisations for centuries. It has mesmerised kings, started wars, and shattered families. In India, gold isn't just a shiny metal; it's status. The more gold you have, the higher you're perceived to be on the social ladder. And this cultural reverence is reflected in the sheer number of jewellery stores dotting every city and town. Somewhere along the way, though, gold was also branded as an 'investment', mostly because its value kept climbing over the years.

Now, a good investment should grow in value, generate an income, and be easy to sell when you need cash. Gold checks only one of these boxes: liquidity. It's easy to sell, sure, but does it grow in value substantially? Not always. Does it give you extra income? Again, not always. So, where does that leave us?

The Trouble with Gold

Let's start with growth. Gold's resale value has increased over time, but unless you're buying it with the clear intention of selling it later, what's the point? Especially when it comes to jewellery. If you're buying jewellery to enjoy it, fantastic. But if you're trying to 'invest' in jewellery, it's a terrible idea. Making charges and wastage make the cost per gram much higher than plain gold coins or bars.

And then there's income—or the lack of it. Gold doesn't pay you dividends like stocks, or interest like fixed deposits. It just sits in your locker, for which you'll probably pay an annual fee. And if you really think about it, 30 grams of gold will still be just 30 grams of gold, no matter how long you hold onto it.

But hey, gold is liquid. You can turn it into cash fairly easily, especially if you're holding coins or bars rather than intricate jewellery pieces. That's where gold shines: stability and liquidity. It's the ultimate 'rainy day' asset.

Therefore, gold, while a stable investment with high liquidity, does not have any scope for growth, nor does it support you with any additional source of income.

But I Must Invest in Gold!

Here's the deal: If you're not planning to sell the gold you're buying, it's not really an investment. It's a keepsake, a cultural statement, or a security blanket. However, gold can be a smart move during certain situations, like periods of high inflation or economic uncertainty. Stocks and bonds may nosedive in value, but gold typically holds steady.

If you want to invest in gold, consider these smarter options:

- ⇨ **Sovereign Gold Bonds (SGBs):** Issued by the government, these bonds are a great alternative to holding physical gold. They offer annual interest (currently around 2.5%), are free from capital gains tax if held until maturity, and don't involve storage worries.
- ⇨ **Digital Gold Platforms:** If you want flexibility and hate the hassle of physical storage, there are a number of fintech apps that now let you buy, sell, and even gift gold digitally in fractional amounts, sometimes as low as ₹10!
- ⇨ **Gold Coins or Bars:** These have lower premiums compared to jewellery and are easier to sell.

It is important to remember that if you're not planning to sell the gold that you're purchasing, it isn't really an 'investment'. However, investing in gold is a good idea when there is inflation abound, or when the economic scenario is unstable, because gold won't lose its value the way shares and stocks will when there is instability.

You're So Golden

Gold's primary role in your portfolio is as a hedge against risk, not as a growth driver. Gold's value may rise over time, but when adjusted for inflation, the real returns aren't exactly dazzling. Meanwhile, well-diversified mutual funds can outpace inflation and generate wealth, so when you're creating your portfolio, make sure you allocate accordingly. Gold might be a strong safety net, but too much of it can suffocate your portfolio.

Side Note: Diamonds Are Not Forever

Diamonds, unlike gold have never really been a true asset class. Natural diamonds are only an investment when they are extremely large (10 carats and upwards), when they are of cultural or historical significance (like Golconda diamonds or if they belonged to Mughal emperors), or have a rare quality of colour. These are the diamonds that get auctioned and sold at high rates. The diamonds that you and I buy, on the other hand, lose value the moment it gets on your hands. With the rising popularity of Lab Grown Diamonds and the aggressive push that the Indian government is giving them, diamonds are only going to lose more value over time. The good news is that it's never been cheaper to get that diamond bracelet you've been lusting after. So, enjoy your diamonds—just don't invest in them.

Real Estate and Why Buying a Home Isn't an Investment

I'll never tire of saying this: Buying a home to live in is not the same as investing in real estate. These are two very different beasts.

So, what's the difference?

At its core, a home is...home. It's where you stay. Where you live. Where you hang your hat, your fancy lights, and your child's first painting. An investment, on the other hand, is something you expect to make money off of. If you're buying a home to live in, you're looking at it through a lens of comfort, locality, and emotional connection. An investment is all about returns, rental yields, and cash flow.

But I Can Always Sell It!

Investments, by definition, are made to generate profit or income. When you're living in the house you've bought, you're not generating income—you're spending money on EMIs, maintenance, and other costs. Sure, you might sell it for a profit someday, but to truly call it an asset, your home needs to be free of emotional attachment.

And wait! If you've bought it with a loan, it's not really 'yours' until that loan is cleared. It's a (future) asset, not an investment today. So, let's spare ourselves the mental gymnastics of trying to make it something it's not.

Your Home Doesn't Need to Be an Investment

Your home is your space. It's stability, and the ability to say, this small patch of land is mine. It's an expensive outgo, yes, but it's one that serves your life, not your portfolio. Buying a home is never a bad idea. Just make sure you go in convinced that it's not about making money—it's about building your life.

Before You Sign That Sale Deed: Questions to Ask Yourself

1. **Can you make a 40% down payment?** I'll be blunt—if you can't make a debt-free down payment of at least 40% of the total cost (or have that amount in savings), you

probably can't afford the place. The cost of a home isn't just the square foot amount, there's at least 10-15% of the home's cost that you'll spend on registration, stamp duty, etc. And if you're able to put down a larger down payment, you've automatically activated smaller EMIs, shorter tenure, and lower interest. Win-win-win.

2. How will this impact your savings and investments? Of course you'll be liquidating a portion of your investments for the down payment, but your EMIs shouldn't wipe out your ongoing savings or leave you financially naked. If buying this home means stretching yourself too thin, hit pause.

3. Do you have a 'What If' plan? Life is unpredictable (remember…2020?). Can you still pay your EMI if the worst happens—a job loss, a medical emergency? Do you have a safety net? If not, think long and hard before committing.

4. Are you cool with the compromises? No home is perfect. Maybe you'll get the space but not the locality, or vice versa. Or you'll get both but at a price that makes you sweat. Be honest with yourself about what you can live with—and what you can't.

The Opportunity Cost of Homeownership

Here's the thing: every rupee you put into buying a home is a rupee you're not investing elsewhere, at a greater rate of return. And while a home gives you stability, it comes with recurring costs like maintenance and taxes that can chip away at your finances.

And whatever you do, don't look at home buying as something that you *have* to do before you hit 40. Do it when you're financially comfortable and can truly afford it. This is a purchase that knocks at least a decade's worth of savings, so consider it very carefully before you dive in.

Buying Property under Construction

When you buy a property that's just under construction, you become eligible for very flexible terms and conditions. Under-construction property enables you to become a 'homeowner' without the burn of high EMIs. Apart from having to pay lower EMIs during the construction period (known as 'Pre EMIs'), you'll also get more flexible payment schedules.

So your EMIs step up gradually, in tandem with the house's construction. The risk, of course, is that the building itself might never materialise. There are a number of housing projects that end up getting delayed, stalled, or just not what they were promised. The Lavasa township in Maharashtra, once promised to be 'India's answer to Portofino', is currently a ghost town. The Unitech Group, which was found guilty of siphoning homeowners' funds and whose owners are now incarcerated, has thousands of homeowners who've paid their dues but are yet to see any apartment materialise.

So while buying under-construction property can be an attractive proposition, don't get swayed by the price tag or the loan terms. Do your research, check the builder's reputation, and be realistic about timelines.

Now Let's Talk about Real Estate Investments

If you're thinking of investing in real estate—either a smaller residential flat to let out as a rental or Airbnb, or a piece of land you can flip at a later date—you're playing an entirely different game. You're looking at metrics like:

- ⇨ **Rental Yield:** How much rental income can this property generate? Short-term rentals (where the tenant stays for only a few days or few months) are much more profitable than longer rental agreements. That said, short-term rentals are more expensive maintenance wise, so your mileage might vary.
- ⇨ **Cap Rate:** If you were to sell this piece of land or building, what would be your return on your investment relative to its cost?
- ⇨ **Market Trends:** Is this an area that will appreciate in the future because of upcoming infrastructure or urbanisation? If you're considering buying a plot of land, for example, it's vital to check market trends. The maintenance cost of plots may be low and the allure of multiplying your investment is high, but if you've read market trends wrong, you might be stuck with a piece of land that just doesn't appreciate. Analysing market trends will also help you understand if you're buying property/land in a place that's at high risk of encroachment, or illegal squatting.

The Tax Benefits of Buying Property

For homebuyers, Indian tax laws allow deductions on home loan interest, which can lighten the financial load. That said, it's capped at ₹2,00,000 per annum (pro tip: If you're buying property as a couple, register the property jointly so both of you can take advantage of the deduction).

Real estate investors can also benefit from this tax break, and claim the deduction on the rental income they earn.

You Don't Have to Buy Property to Invest in Real Estate

If owning any kind of property feels overwhelming but you're still interested in real estate, say hello to REITs (Real Estate Investment Trusts). REITs are like mutual funds for real estate and are generally managed by prestigious builders. They pool money from multiple investors and invest in income-generating properties like commercial offices, shopping centres, and hotels.

Why Consider REITs? For starters, the entry is far more democratic. You can start with as little as a few thousand rupees. What's more, REITs are traded on stock exchanges, so you can buy and sell your units with the same ease and convenience that you would shares.

These instruments allow you to diversify your portfolio without the hassle of actually owning properties. An REIT can even pay dividends from the rental income it earns, giving you the option to earn passive income from them. REITs are currently very nascent in India—there are fewer than 10 as I write this in 2024—but there is immense potential for this asset class to rise over the years. After all, India is the fastest growing REIT market in the Asia Pacific!

Play the Long Game

Buying a home is a marathon, not a sprint. It's okay to wait until you're financially ready. The market's not running away, and rushing into a purchase can leave you stuck with regrets (and stress). Take your time. This decision should enhance your life—not overwhelm it. And hey, if you're not ready? That's okay. The right home—or investment—will wait for you.

Alternative Investments

Cryptocurrency

If we want to evaluate cryptocurrency as an investment, it's important that we understand *what* it is, starting with blockchain.

Imagine you're in a group chat where everyone is constantly keeping tabs on what's being said. Every message is double-checked by the entire group before it's locked in, and once it's in, it can't be changed and it *definitely* can't be deleted. That's basically blockchain—a giant, super-secure, tamper-proof group chat for transactions.

These blockchains are public record and are totally **decentralised.** Understanding this term, matters. What is decentralisation? It means that no one party has control over the blockchain where crypto transactions are recorded. There are no banks, no governments, no regulatory bodies—

no one—who controls transaction history. All transaction information is maintained by multiple parties across the world. And when everyone has access, no one has control.

This lack of control is vital, because Cryptocurrency itself is like digital cash—but without the paper, the coins, or even a government backing it, like traditional currencies. Crypto exists purely as code on the internet, stored on the blockchain that keeps track of who owns what. Unlike regular money (rupees, dollars, euros), which is controlled by central banks, crypto is verified by a network of computers around the world.

At its core, **crypto is just information**—a string of encrypted transactions proving that you own a certain amount of digital currency. But because this information is verified by thousands of computers instead of a single authority, it's nearly impossible to fake or duplicate.

But is it a currency in the traditional sense? Not at all. It's not accepted widely (which is a core requirement for any currency) and its value fluctuates far too wildly.

So how is its value decided? Through scarcity and trust. Just like gold or silver, which people agree has value because it's rare and hard to mine, crypto gains value when enough people believe in it. Bitcoin, for example, has a limited supply of 21 million coins—so as demand grows, its price goes up. Other cryptocurrencies have similarly limited supply.

Cryptocurrencies were once very niche playing grounds, and even the knowledge of crypto was restricted to smaller tech circles. To say things have changed would be an understatement. The pandemic blew cryptocurrency into mainstream consciousness—to the point where governments have made it a part of financial policymaking. President Donald Trump announced his second term by launching his own token (TRUMP) and signalling a new era for cryptocurrencies.

The startling highs and crippling lows of crypto from its mainstream acceptance in 2020 to its great fall in 2022 have left a lot of investors scarred—or at the very least, nauseous. Now, as a pro-crypto world leader emerges, will things change?

Let me start by saying that just because something is trendy, doesn't mean it's good for you, or even meant for you. Investing blindly is one of the worst personal finance mistakes you can make. It's vital to be able to anticipate potential outcomes before you invest even a rupee of your money in something.

Decentralisation Is Not for Beginners

Cryptocurrencies don't exist in the real world. There are no coins, no notes, no physical representation of money. The only proof of you having cryptocurrency is that password protected wallet—so how does one verify authenticity? How do they make sure they're not being duped? This is where the blockchain comes in.

A blockchain is a continuously growing list of records that is controlled by peer-to-peer networks—basically, there is an objective, opinion-free record of every cryptocurrency transaction in the world which is maintained by multiple parties all at the same time—the super secure groupchat we spoke about in the previous page.

Another way to think about blockchains is to imagine them to be school public address or announcement systems. You go up to the mike and say that you, X, are giving the coin(s) from your wallet to Y. The people listening (the peer-to-peer network) take note of the transaction together and presto! You've just sold crypto. Y's wallet will now show the coins that she received from you.

Why am I taking the time and effort to explain blockchain so many times? My friend, you need to know this because when shit hits the fan, you have no one to complain to. There is data to show that losses from cryptocurrency-related frauds and scams increased 45% in 2023 from 2022, totalling more than $5.6 billion. And in 2024, cryptocurrency users suffered losses surpassing $1.2 billion due to scams and exploits.[2]

If you fall prey to something and lose your money, there's really little to nothing that can be done. No managers you can send an angry letter to. Is this something you're okay with? Are you savvy enough to spot genuine crypto opportunities from Nigerian Bitcoin Princes? Because if you're not, you really shouldn't be putting money in crypto.

India Hates Crypto

India as an economy is very wary of crypto. We are a young, digital first, money hungry economy. Naturally, we are ripe for crypto—and its scams. This is why current regulations around crypto are complex and very unfriendly to anyone trying to run a cryptocurrency exchange in

India. Exchanges are required to mandatorily do KYC, there is a cryptocurrency bill in the works, and overall, the government is trying everything it can do to control crypto, which is massively anticlimactic to the values of decentralisation and independence on which crypto was founded.

Finally, the tax on crypto is way harsher than any other asset class in the country—in fact, it's taxed the same way lottery winnings are. You've to pay 30% on any gain or income you may have received from crypto, with an additional 1% TDS that the exchange has to deduct on transactions exceeding ₹50,000 annually.

In today's world, things change. Quick. But if you are tempted by the promises of crypto, by all means, go ahead. But don't fool yourself into thinking you're investing. You're gambling.

Art and Collectibles

Art and collectibles (including NFTs) are a fast-growing asset class that don't follow the rules of the market, but I'll be honest with you—neither of them is for beginners. They're very niche, which means finding buyers/sellers is a complex, time-consuming process. Art is also very subjective and requires deep expertise. If you aren't a connoisseur, this is an area you want to stay away from.

Expensive Is Not an Investment

Sometimes it feels like we live in an age where anything and everything can be an investment. Gold, investment. But also, sneakers, dresses, handbags, and even lipsticks. While I am all for the mainstreaming of finance language, it can become dangerous if we delude ourselves into believing that if something is expensive, then it must be an investment.

On most days, that's all they are—expensive. I won't deny that there may be 'returns' to some of these things. A Rolex or a designer handbag, perhaps, could open doors that were previously not open. But it's vital for you, as a buyer, to know the difference between an 'expensive' piece and an 'investment' piece. It's okay to buy expensive things. Just stop calling them investments.

When the Tax Man Comes A-Calling

When you invest, you get to own assets. It could be a home, it could be mutual funds. But they're *assets*. And they're yours. Now, as we've established before, investments allow you to do 2 things: Derive income from them or give you growth in value.

When you receive income from an investment—whether it's interest or rent—the taxation is fairly straightforward. When you sell your investment for a profit, on the other hand, you'll attract capital gains tax.

Short-Term and Long-Term Assets and Gains

In 2024, the Indian government simplified the taxation of capital assets. If you own an asset (real estate, stocks, mutual funds, bonds) for *less than 12 months*, it becomes a Short-Term Asset.

If you own an asset for *longer than 12 months*, it becomes a Long-Term Asset.

Your gains (Sale Value reduced by Cost) on selling Short-Term Assets will be taxed at 20%, and your gains on selling Long-Term Assets will be at 12.5% *provided* your gains are in excess of ₹1.25 lakh. So, up to ₹1.25 lakh of gains is tax free on long-term assets, but your gains over and above this amount will be taxed at 12.5%.

Go Forth and Invest—The TL; DR

This was a heavy chapter, I won't lie. And I'd like for you to revisit this every time you're trying to invest in something new. Remember, garam masala recipes take years and many iterations to perfect. They also evolve with time and taste. Don't try to go for the perfect recipe in your first go—just start. As time progresses, you'll find what works and what doesn't. What matters is that you don't stop grinding, er, investing.

Here's what I want you to take away:

Understand Your 'Why'

Before you dive into investing, define your financial goals. Be as specific as possible—whether it's a family trip to Spain, your child's education, or buying a home. A clear 'why' keeps you focused and prevents you from falling for FOMO investing.

Be SMART about Your Goals

Your financial goals should be Specific, Measurable, Achievable, Relevant, and Time-bound (SMART). For example, instead of saying, 'I want to save,' say, 'I will save ₹30,000 per month for 12 months for a ₹3.6 lakh vacation.'

Can You Handle This

Not all investments are for everyone, which is why you need to know your risk profile. Your risk profile depends on your financial obligations, personality, and life stage.

Debt investments (like bonds) offer stable returns but limited growth. Equity investments (like stocks) have higher potential returns but come with greater risk. The balance between the two should align with your goals.

Mutual Funds Sahi Hai

Mutual funds pool money from investors and invest in different asset classes. Systematic Investment Plans (SIPs) let you invest small amounts regularly, making it easier to build wealth over time.

Gold Isn't Always Golden

Gold can act as a 'safety net' during economic instability, but it doesn't generate income. Instead of buying jewellery, consider gold bonds or digital gold for better liquidity and fewer additional costs.

Let's Get Real Estate

Your home is not an 'investment' unless it generates income (like rental yield). Think of it as a lifestyle purchase, not a money-making venture. Real estate investments, like rental properties or REITs (Real Estate Investment Trusts), require a strategic approach.

Alt Not Always Right

Alternative investments like cryptocurrency can be highly volatile and is often more gambling than investing. It's decentralised, which means no one can help you recover funds if something goes wrong. India's regulations and taxes on crypto are also strict.

Art, collectibles, and NFTs may sound appealing, but they're niche and often require expert knowledge. For beginners, it's better to focus on more mainstream asset classes.

Notes

1. Nikhil Agarwal, 'F&O Addiction: 1.1 Crore traders lost 1.8 lakh crore in 3 years reveals SEBI study', *The Economic Times*, 25 September 2024. https://economictimes.indiatimes.com/markets/stocks/news/fo-addiction-1-1-crore-traders-lost-rs-1-8-lakh-crore-in-3-years-reveals-sebi-study/articleshow/113599317.cms
2. Hannah Lang, 'Losses from crypto scams grew 45% in 2023', *Reuters*, 10 September 2024. https://www.reuters.com/technology/losses-crypto-scams-grew-45-2023-fbi-says-2024-09-09/

Q&A: Vivek Kaul

Vivek Kaul is a writer, economic commentator, and author of five books, including the bestselling *Easy Money* trilogy on the history of money and banking and how that caused the financial crisis that started in 2008. Kaul is a regular columnist for *Mint, BBC, Dainik Jagran, Firstpost, Bangalore Mirror,* and *The Deccan Herald* and has also appeared as an economics commentator on *BBC, Mirror Now, CNBC Awaaz,* and *NDTV*. He speaks regularly on economics and finance and has lectured at IIM Bangalore, IIM Indore, IIM Kozhikode, IIM Visakhapatnam, NMIMS, and the Symbiosis Institute of Media and Communication, among others. Kaul lives in Mumbai and loves reading crime fiction in his free time.

1. You've witnessed three distinct financial generations in India—*post-liberalisation* (the first generation with access to new consumer markets), *post-internet* (the digital native), and *post-social media* (the social media native). What are the defining financial traits of each of these generations? As we charge ahead into the future (Generation Alpha, they

say, is about to step into adulthood), do you think money habits are getting progressively better? Or progressively worse?

Vivek: I dislike the word 'generations'. All these so-called generations have had their own wild rides in the stock market. There was the Harshad Mehta scam in the early 90s, the Ketan Parekh scam in the early 2000s, and in between there was the vanishing-companies scam where companies would go for an IPO, raise money, and disappear.

There was a big stock market crash in 2008, and people stayed away from the market altogether. And now we have the current generation, which is suddenly confused about the stock market crashing, because they'd believed that it would just go up perpetually.

Most people who invest don't seem to understand the basics and get carried away by the flavour of the season, or by whatever so-called experts seem to be saying.

The only distinction I'd like to make is that in the earlier era, it wasn't easy for pseudo experts to reach out to people. But today anyone with a mobile phone can have an audience—and it feels like the flakier you are, the bigger your audience!

I guess what I'm trying to say is that irrespective of the generation we are referring to, most investors just want to hear things that are crisp, confident-sounding, and want to be told that it's easy to get rich quick and fast. And irrespective of which generation you belong to, if this is the approach, you'll get taken to the cleaners.

2. You write a lot about loss aversion in your newsletters. Is this the behavioural economic theory that you believe is most important for consumers to understand? If you were to list down 2-3 behaviours that investors need to watch out for, what would they be?

Vivek: More than behaviours, what investors (both young and old) don't seem to realise is that it's not possible to get rich quickly through investing. You need a couple of decades to get there. And most of us make a limited amount of money.

Most people believe the trend they're seeing will stay on forever. So, if the markets are up, they don't see the possibility of a drop. And the media also tends to highlight only success stories. So when someone sees a successful investor they immediately think, hey I can do this too. You won't hear the stories of people failing.

Survivorship bias and the understanding that investing is not a route to overnight wealth are what people need to know.

3. After half a decade of what felt like a never-ending bull run, we are now entering the zone where things aren't as shiny as they may have seemed, and the exuberance is coming down. You'd written about how the Indian markets were a self-sustaining Ponzi scheme and it does look like we're hurtling towards a more uncertain future. What are some of the basic principles you think that investors should remember as the tides turn? Should first time/young investors approach this differently from those who've been investing in the market since 2020?

Vivek: The basic principles of investing don't change—whether it's in 2020 or 2025. The most important principle is diversification. You need to split your money not only across asset classes, but also within asset classes. But psychologically, this is hard to follow. When the markets were going up, and stock prices were shooting up, a lot of people made money in the markets. So at that point, it takes a lot of psychological maturity to *not* go all in and stand by your risk profile.

Take someone like me, I'm a freelance writer. I don't have a pension, and my income is quite unpredictable. It doesn't make sense for me to bet all my investments on the stock market because there's no predicting how things will go. The downside is that yes, I'll miss out on some gains.

Another example is gold, which is really hot right now, and all the influencers are talking about it. While there's really no telling if gold prices can go further up, the real time to have invested in gold was in 2019, 2020, when prices weren't high. Had you followed a diversification strategy then, you'd have stood to gain from gold's rise now. In fact, anyone who'd diversified wouldn't have seen their portfolio drop the way equity investors are seeing theirs drop.

There's too much noise around the business of investing and too many people who make it seem complex because they stand to make money from managing yours.

So yes, my advice is to stick to the basics and not put all your eggs into one basket.

4. If you could give only one piece of financial advice to a 25-year-old today, what would it be?

Vivek: You cannot get rich quickly by investing.

In my mind, there are only 3 ways to get rich quickly. The first is by stealing, the second is an unexpected inheritance, and the third is to be lucky enough where your business idea gets funded by a venture capitalist. In these 3 situations you can get rich quickly—exceptions apply, of course.

When you invest, on the other hand, you cannot get rich quickly.

Let me give you an example: When Bitcoin was at its peak in 2021, I wrote a piece about how I'd never buy Bitcoin. A lot of Bitcoin believers wrote to me saying, 'Have fun being poor.' Here's the thing: Yes, bitcoin prices went up, but how many people became wealthy because of that? You might have invested some Rs. 10,000 which would've become Rs. 20,000, or maybe even Rs. 25,000. But you didn't become wealthy.

In the last few years, many finfluencers have come around and promoted the idea that you can become rich quickly through stocks and derivatives. Now, these finfluencers became rich because they sold these ideas through courses and sponsorships, not because of the money they made through investing in stocks and derivatives.

A lot of people also go gaga when someone—like a stock market guru—makes money in the market. But a lot of these gurus started investing in the 1980s. They became rich at a fast pace, yes, but not overnight.

Finally, most stock market stories carry survivorship bias. It's a situation where only success, and successful people get highlighted. So while many of us would've wanted to become rich through the stock market, not everyone's is a success story.

5. Slightly philosophical—what do you think is the greatest enemy of financial security, in today's times?

Vivek: The first enemy would be the lack of any particularly useful skill which the market is ready to pay for at any point in time. If you're not in a position to make money because you don't have skill that the market values at any given point, then that is the first enemy of financial security.

Now, assuming that someone is skilled, and has a skill that the market values that will not become outdated in today's fast paced world, what's the biggest threat to their financial security?

In their case—and this might sound funny—I think it is the smartphone. I say this because of multiple reasons. It's been proven—and this is backed by research—that when you spend digitally, and you don't spend cash, you actually end up spending more. There is a certain pain that's associated with spending cash that doesn't exist when you spend digitally. The research was initially carried out on credit cards, but now we're well beyond the age of credit cards. At least the credit cards back in the day were only restricted for a small section of the population. Then came debit cards and now with UPI...it's become very easy to spend.

And that ease of spending is one of the reasons responsible for the fact that household financial savings have fallen in the recent past.

There is another reason why smartphones are detrimental to financial security. Earlier, when you'd invested in stocks or mutual funds, you couldn't really check the value of your investments easily. You had to log into the websites individually to understand what your investments were valued at.

Today, everything can be seen on your phone at a tap of a button. And the interfaces today are so user friendly that you end up checking the value of your investments daily.

This also goes against the overall philosophy of building wealth in the long term. Let's say as we talk, the markets are falling, and you can see the moment you log in to any of your investment apps that the value of your portfolio is falling in comparison to where it probably was yesterday or the day before, and that creates anxiety to sell.

On the flipside, when the markets were going up, and if you hadn't invested in equities and you saw everything going up, that would also create anxiety. And you could end up taking a large bet when equities were at their peak, or overvalued.

So yes, the first enemy would be the lack of a skill that the market values at any point in time or the inability to adapt or learn skills that the market values. The second is the smartphone.

6

Love and Money

Love Doesn't Cost a Thing

To talk about the cost of love and the price of relationships feels wrong, doesn't it? Like throwing bleach on roses. What does one gain by throwing money into matters of the heart anyway?

Everything.

When I got together with my husband, I was practising in my father's Chartered Accountancy firm. Three months into the marriage, I filed his taxes, which meant that I had access to his bank accounts, credit card statements, bills, loan history…everything. But it still took me six more months to actually talk to him about money.

The reason I say this is because I was a finance professional with full access to my partner's money history, and yet I stalled, stammered, overthought, rehearsed conversations in my head a hundred times before I continued to stay silent…the whole shebang. It's hard talking to the ones you love about money.

Years and years of conditioning, societal beliefs, and pop culture have us believing that it is incorrect to discuss money with those you love and yet, it is the number one thing that couples argue about. Money has ruined relationships, ended marriages, and broken homes. But the taboo around discussing finances with partners—both current and potential—continues to exist. As a result, when money does get discussed, it's too little, or worse, too late.

But it shouldn't be this way. Healthy relationships are all about transparency and honesty—especially when it comes to money and the ways in which we approach it. If you haven't yet started talking about money with your partner, now is the time. After all, if you can get naked with someone, you can one hundred percent talk to them about money.

When Should I Start Talking to My Partner about Money?

If you're seeing someone and haven't yet broached the topic of money as yet, think about why you want to talk about it. Our approach to money is almost an extended version of our personalities, shaped and structured by our upbringing, our environments, and even our trauma. Is it a side you're willing to reveal? Is this relationship serious enough for you to broach what is perceived to be a sensitive topic? Would the outcomes of this conversation change the course of your relationship? If the answer to any of these questions is yes, then you should definitely have this conversation. Alternatively, if you've never broached this topic with your partner of x years, start now. The earlier you start talking about money, the better.

Be warned, though. It won't be easy, even if—*especially* if—you're madly in love with each other. The first few times you broach the topic, it will be awkward, uncomfortable and you may even find yourself cringing, physically, to give your opinions on what you think about the other's spending habits or to even talk about the goings on of each other's bank statements. But I promise you that the more you talk about it, the easier it becomes, and the stronger you will see your relationship becoming. Honesty is the key to success in any relationship! And if you're not going to be honest about your money, there isn't much left to be honest about.

Ok, But How *Do I Actually Talk to Them about Money?*

While I'd say that it's best to be straightforward about money from the very beginning, you can adopt different approaches depending on how long you've been with your partner. If you've been seeing them for only a little while, the topics you bring up can be lighter, but with a clear emphasis on money. Here are a few examples:

'Hey, I've been meaning to tell you, can we meet at the other cafe instead of this one? The menu is really expensive and I can't afford it on the regular.'

'Hey, would it be okay if we met at the other restaurant from next time? I'd prefer it if we went to nicer places, even if it's more expensive.'

'What do you think of this brand? I like their technology but it's really expensive when compared to what's out there.'

The idea is to ease into conversations about money. But if you've been with your partner for a while, cut straight to the chase at a time when you're both relaxed and present. A simple, 'Hey, I want to talk to you about our finances' is all you need to say. Avoid using the words 'I think' or 'maybe'. You've thought about this enough! And 9 out of 10 times, you'll find your partner ready and willing to get right into the conversation. If they're not ready, ask them for a time and place to bring it up again. *Make* time for it.

What *Do I Talk to Them About?*

When you're planning to spend the rest of your life with someone, nothing is off the table. But if you're looking for a place to begin, here are a few ideas (in no particular order):

1. **Money Values:** How does my partner think about and process money? Is it a big deal for them? Or do they not think about it at all? Do they think about money the same way that I do? And is that even a good thing?

2. **Debt History:** Have either of you taken loans? Are you done paying it off? Are they done paying it off? What are your EMIs like every month?

3. **Familial Obligations:** Do you or your partner have parents or anyone else who is solely dependent on you/ them? What's the monthly outgo like? Is it a situation that's temporary or is it something that will prevail in the long term?

4. **Salaries:** Talk about how much you make in a month. Do you have stable incomes? Who makes more? What's

the difference in pay? How will this impact your/their contribution to your lives together?

5. Savings: How are you saving? What are you saving in? What does your partner save in? Are you saving enough? Do you follow the same principles?

6. Spending Habits: Are you thrifty? Or do you have a lifestyle? What about your partner? Are they the same? Could differences in spending habits have an impact on your relationship?

7. Career Path: What is the career path that you have planned for yourself? What is your partner's? How will this impact your finances? For example, someone who's salaried now might want to get into entrepreneurship in the near future, which might require a significant outgo and bring in temporarily unstable incomes.

8. Bank Accounts: Do both of you have your own accounts? Do you need a joint account at all? If you do have a joint account, who operates it?

9. Credit Cards and Bills: How many credit cards do you have? What are your bills on average? How do you intend to split bills if you've a future together? If your incomes are very far apart, for example, a 50-50 split would be unfair.

10. Future Plans: What you want to save for—maybe you have an entrepreneurial dream. Or even a dream kitchen. A specific school you want your child to go to. A specific school that you want to go to. A dream house. Talk about all your aspirations!

This is by no means an exhaustive list. But it is a good way to get the conversation started. And before you start talking about these with your partner, try answering these questions yourself! You may feel queasy, especially if these are things you're actively thinking about for the first time. Get used to it though, because the more time you spend articulating your own financial situation, the easier it gets to talk about—with your partner or with anyone else.

A Note on Transparency and Privacy

Yes, it is important to be honest and open about money, but transparency doesn't translate into sharing, and in return, expecting your partner to share every single detail of their everyday transactions. You shouldn't have to share the nitty-gritty of your statements either. The idea is to know and understand your partner's financial position and build trust. And trust cannot be built without respecting your partner's privacy.

Yours, Mine, Ours

Confession: My husband and I opened a joint bank account together 8 whole years after we got together. While we were transparent about our finances, it took us opening the joint account to see how our totally sterile approach was far less efficient than we believed it to be. And that's the thing about money and relationships—extremes rarely work out. Total dependence on one joint account, in fact, is more inefficient than two separate accounts. So try to achieve a middle ground that helps both of you live your lives as

YOURS, MINE & OURS

Item	Yours	Mine	Ours
Bank Accounts	Individual Bank Account, Bank Locker	Individual Bank Account, Bank Locker	Joint Bank Account
Insurance	Term Life Insurance	Term Life Insurance	Health Insurance [Family Floater], Insurance Investments
Expenses	Personal & Discretionary Expenses	Personal & Discretionary Expenses	Joint living and child related expenses

Item	Yours	Mine	Ours
Investments	Personal Portfolio	Personal Portfolio	Large investments that both parties contribute to, ex: Real Estate
Debt	Pre-relationship debt, personal credit card	Pre-relationship debt, personal credit card	EMIs for joint assets and expenses, joint credit cards
Other Assets	Inheritance, assets (gold, art etc) purchased in your name.	Inheritance, assets (gold, art etc) purchased in your name.	Assets purchased jointly

individuals as well as a couple. I'd recommend looking at your finances through three parallel tracks—yours, mine, and ours.

Who Pays for What?

When there are clear disparities between your income and your partner's, sharing should be equitable, not equal. So, expenses are best split in the proportion of each partner's earnings simply because it's not fair to split halfway when one partner is making considerably more than the other. Alternatively, each partner can assume responsibility for one type of expense. You could cover rent, for example, while your partner covers groceries.

If you're a freelancer or someone whose income streams aren't predictable, it's not unusual to feel the pressure of 'contributing' towards the household. If you're open with your partner about this, both of you can figure out a system that works for you. Maybe you take care of certain expenses entirely when inflows are good. Maybe you contribute in proportion to the minimum amount of income you bring in. If you're on a sabbatical or just not working, remember that contributing, physically, to your household is just as valuable as income contribution.

Taking care of a household, especially a household with children, is an unpaid economic activity and holds great value. Do not let anyone tell you otherwise. On the flip side, there is a certain pressure that men continue to feel when it comes to 'taking care' of their partners and to be the primary bread winner of the family.

All I'll say is that we're 25 years into the 21st century. It's time to let go of the notion that your gender determines the role you play in your relationship or that you must draw a certain salary to fulfil the ones you love. As long as both of you are able to arrive at money decisions together, openly and in ways that make both of you feel comfortable and valued, you're doing very well.

Red Flags to Watch Out For

If you're not feeling good about the financial situation in your relationship, it's likely that there are red flags lurking. A red flag is a warning sign of behaviour that is potentially dangerous to your relationship. Money-related red flags should be taken seriously, or at the very least, discussed through during the early stages of the relationship, because they're almost always the starting point for destructive behaviour that can permanently damage your relationship. Here are the most common money-related red flags:

1. *They Avoid Talking about Money*

Does your partner actively avoid talking about money even when you want to? While raising the topic of money in a relationship can be challenging, the awkwardness dissipates after the first few times when your partner considers money with the same importance that you do—even if their strategies for saving and spending are different. But, if you're constantly met with 'no, not now', or 'why do we have to talk about this' or a flat out, 'I'm not interested in talking about money with you', consider it a red flag. It's not even about them having monumental debt or a serious issue with their finances—it's simply the fact that they don't want to be transparent with you.

2. *They're Selective about Their Money Conversations*

Some partners are very opinionated about money when it comes to others but furtive when it comes to their own. If your partner has loud opinions on how you ought to spend your money but changes the topic when it comes to theirs, it's a red flag. There are many variants when it comes to selectiveness—some partners take loans with their joint accounts in such a way that only one takes the brunt of the EMI. Some others don't reveal their income streams. I have heard horror stories where partners have held 'secret' bank accounts, denied the other access to their savings, and were even running parallel households!

3. *They Use Money to Make You Feel Like Shit*

If your partner uses money as a hook to make you feel terrible about yourself, that's a red flag. None of us are perfect with our spending habits, and while healthy discussions and constructive criticism should be welcomed in a relationship, gaslighting and borderline abuse shouldn't be.

Here's an example of what healthy feedback looks like: 'Hey, I noticed that you've been shopping a lot this month. What's happening? We should talk about it because the credit card bill this month looks crazy.'

On the other hand, this is what gaslighting looks like:

'You just don't know how to handle money and you're always wasting it on useless garbage! How can you be so stupid?!'

4. *They Don't See the Point in Independent Accounts*

If your partner doesn't want you to have your own bank accounts or wants you to shut down your existing independent accounts, consider it a glaring financial red flag. While it does make sense to have joint accounts for joint expenses, insisting that you don't need your own account (even if you want or already have one) is an early sign of control. The need for control is often the first sign of abuse in a relationship. And financial abuse, where one partner is practically denied access to money…is very real.

5. *Or They're Totally Exclusionary*

If your partner keeps you out of all their financial decisions, you've got yourself a glaring red flag. While it's totally normal to sneak in a few extra items to your cart without telling your significant other, entering into large transactions or committing to serious debt isn't. Some partners also go ahead with large asset purchases during the course of the relationship but don't include their partner's name in the property documents (while the EMI might go out of the joint account!). Exclusion isn't merely unhealthy, it's also dangerous. The partners being excluded might find themselves in unpleasant parties they had no idea they were invited to.

6. *They Have Abnormal Spending Habits*

If your partner's spending habits are not (somewhat) rational, consider it a red flag. There is plenty that can be said about money and mental health. Spending habits that are consistently off the rails is a red flag of more serious and deep rooted issues. Lavish gifting, spending on things you know they can't afford, overextending to friends and family by way of loans are all warning signs. Alternatively, not wanting to come out at all or refusing to spend are also warning signs. This particular red flag is very instinct led and sometimes people choose to ignore it, but it can come back to haunt you in a way that's far worse if you don't address it as early as possible.

7. *They Need 'Permission' to Take Money Decisions*

The need for permission is a uniquely Indian red flag and probably the most prevalent. While this may seem primarily like a male thing, I'd argue that adults asking for permission is not a good look for any gender (all privilege disclaimers apply). If your partner lives in a joint family system, chances are that there is no hygiene when it comes to their finances and everything goes into one big pot. It's likely that separate accounts or joint accounts with partners are even discouraged. So even the simplest of money decisions require 'permission'. While well-meaning advice and consultations with family are totally acceptable, a roadblock to your financial decision-making process isn't. The moment the word 'permission', or 'I've to ask my parents', or 'I don't take care of these things, my family does', comes up, it's a red, red flag.

Disagreements Are Not a Red Flag

Disagreements when it comes to money are very, very common and if your disagreement was born out of discussion, then they're welcome. My husband and I disagree on a wide spectrum of financial concepts. When it comes to investing, for example, I am very aggressive with my bets.

I invest almost entirely in equity while he's a fixed deposit kind of guy. His conservative approach comes from the fact that his billings as a legal professional are not always predictable, whereas I draw a fixed salary. So what do we do? Compromise. We save individually, transparently, and invest in what we believe in. We take the advice of professionals who know better than us.

When we save for a common goal, whether it's a holiday or for our child's education, we try to arrive at a middle ground. It's usually an instrument that's safer than what I'd like and less conservative than what he's used to. We try to make our choices palatable for the other. When it comes to holidays, for example, I am the kind that would like to spend on premium tickets whereas he would rather spend on experiences at our destination. To make the premium tickets palatable, I collect credit card points that can be used for upgrades. Today, my husband has a credit card specifically for collecting airmiles! Things work out when you can convince your spouse of the value you see in what you spend.

The Great Indian Joint Family

I cannot talk about money and marriage in an Indian context without talking about the Great Indian Joint Family^{TM}. I grew up in a really large family. My mother was the last of seven siblings and my maternal grandmother lived with us. This meant that our household resembled the sets of a low-budget Sooraj Barjatya movie and was constantly overflowing with uncles, aunts, and cousins to the point where I was convinced that there was no other way to live. The joint family setup, where generations of families live under the same roof, was expected to have reduced as urbanisation set in. But has it, really? For the bulk of urban Indians, rising housing and living costs, the increase in the number of women at the workplace and the need for childcare/elder care have resulted in an increase of joint families or intergenerational families. Between 2001 and 2011, joint families in urban India grew 29% whereas in rural areas it only grew by 2%. Joint families are also 4 times more prevalent in the north of India than in the south.[1]

It's worth mentioning that although the very model of the joint family has evolved, it's not any less challenging to navigate. I know progressive joint families where everyone co-exists without getting into each other's business and I know old-school households that possess incredible amounts of wealth, but expect their daughters-in-law to not work and ask permission for every single transaction that they intend to make. It is truly the slipperiest of all slopes.

Joint families come with intense social pressure and operate with a great deal of stealth. I know women who had no clue of what they were signing up for, only to realise that they had practically no financial backing until it was too late. I also know of men who want to live more independently and pursue their own entrepreneurial dreams, but continue to stay with their families and family businesses because freedom comes at the cost of burning, or at the very least, charring bridges.

So What's One to Do?

At the outset, know that there is no perfect system for co-existing. While joint families can cramp yo' style if you're a young couple, living alone can be incredibly challenging if you're young parents (as demonstrated by the pandemic) and the joint family system can bring in much needed support.

Besides, it's entirely possible to have zero control over your money while living only with your partner (or even alone!) and having full financial independence while living with your in-laws. So while the system has its own set of pros and cons, you can always make it work for you, simply by communicating what you want. If you find yourself shot down though, you should not hesitate to take things into your own hands.

Money and Unconventional Families

On the other spectrum of joint families are unconventional family setups and same-sex relationships. How are they to navigate their finances together? While the broad guidelines remain the same, opening up joint bank accounts for both same-sex couples and couples who are living in together, can be a hassle.

This is despite the fact that the RBI, which is the authority when it comes to banking in India, explicitly states that any two individuals can open a joint bank account. The bottleneck lies with the banks themselves, that are wary of unconventional relationships. Opening a bank account for heterosexual couples who are living together, and same-sex couples, can be stressful and time-consuming, with both additional paperwork and unnecessary jibes. Much like getting comfortable with the idea of living together or same-sex relationships, access to the same financial tools that married couples possess will take time.

This Is What Financial Abuse Looks Like

Financial abuse is a very legitimate form of abuse where one partner exerts control over the other using money. It is the ultimate culmination of all the red flags we spoke about earlier and is recognised as a form of domestic violence. There are many forms of financial abuse, including:

1. Taking full control over combined finances and actively preventing the other partner from accessing any bank account.
2. Asking for minute details with respect to the other partner's spending and making them beg for money.
3. Punishing your partner by depriving them of money even for the most basic needs.

4. Preventing and actively blocking any scenario that might make the other partner financially independent, such as jobs or entrepreneurship opportunities.
5. Capturing any and all of the other partner's assets, like gold or any other property they might have.
6. Locking away the other partner's important financial documents including PAN cards and other bank certificates.
7. Constant demands and threats for money.

There are varying degrees of financial abuse, but sadly, it has been normalised to a large extent in India. There have been multiple accounts of highly educated families and husbands going to the extent of murdering their daughters-in-law/wives for the sake of a greater dowry.

A story I haven't been able to get out of my head for years now involves a 25-year-old Chartered Accountant who was murdered by her in-laws so that their son (who was a doctor! A doctor!) could remarry for more money.[2] I also remember the flurry that the story created on social media and the number of people who said, 'But she was a CA! Why didn't she just walk away from the marriage?' Here's the thing though—if you're not from the 1% that had a forward upbringing, upper-middle class peers, and parents who taught you the value of independence, walking away is not an option.

Divorce Continues to Carry a Great Deal of Stigma, Even among Urban Indians

As a result of our circumstances growing up (for a lot of us), and social conditioning, women who are subject to financial abuse continue to suffer in silence. If you notice a friend, relative, or acquaintance whose money behaviour has suddenly undergone a dramatic shift after they've entered a new relationship, please talk to them about it. There are a number of NGOs in the country that are actively helping victims of abuse get help, so you can also help connect them to the person in need.

Money Can't Buy You Love

But it can get you freedom. Talking, and at times, even thinking about money in the context of a relationship is uncomfortable and challenging. But instead of looking at money as an impediment in your relationship, think of it as…a fertiliser. Yeah, it's smelly and hard to handle, but if you don't fertilise your garden, you don't get to enjoy the roses.

Love and Money—The TL; DR

Here's what I want you to take away from this chapter:

Love Isn't Cheap

Money is one of the biggest sources of conflict for couples. And it's never 'too early' or 'too late' to talk about finances in a relationship. Whether you're casually dating or preparing for a long-term commitment, discussing money sooner rather than later can strengthen the relationship.

Baby Steps

Start small if you're in a new relationship—mentioning budgeting preferences or expenses in everyday life can open the door. Speaking about money often eases conversations over time.

There's Enough to Talk About

- ⇨ Money Values: Are you savers or spenders?
- ⇨ Debt: What loans and EMIs do you both have?
- ⇨ Obligations: Who else depends on your income?
- ⇨ Salaries, Savings, and Future Plans: Are your incomes steady? Any big career changes planned?
- ⇨ Joint vs. Separate Accounts: What goes in what?
- ⇨ Sharing the Load: How do you plan to split bills and future investments?

Are You Oversharing?

While transparency is important, you don't need to disclose every tiny transaction. The goal is to build trust while respecting each other's financial independence.

Stand Together Separately

A balanced approach to finances as a couple involves three buckets:

- ⇨ Yours: Their personal bank accounts, personal debts, and individual investments.
- ⇨ Mine: Your accounts, debts, and investments.
- ⇨ Ours: Shared expenses, joint savings, and big-ticket investments.

These Flags Are Red

- ⇨ Avoiding money talks altogether.
- ⇨ Controlling financial decisions or withholding financial information.
- ⇨ Abnormal spending patterns, whether extreme frugality or splurging beyond means.
- ⇨ Partners needing 'permission' for basic financial decisions due to external family dynamics.

Financial Abuse Is Real

Financial abuse happens when one partner uses money to exert control—restricting access to funds, making their partner beg for money, or blocking them from becoming financially independent. This behaviour is often normalised in Indian households, but know that it's abuse.

Notes

1. TNN, 'Why Joint Families Are Back in Urban India', *The Times of India*, 16 July 2017. https://timesofindia.indiatimes.com/home/sunday-times/why-joint-families-are-back-in-urban-india/articleshow/59614752.cms
2. Pheba Mathew, 'They tortured her, we kept sending her back: Family distraught after CA killed in TN over dowry', *The News Minute*, 31 July 2017. https://www.thenewsminute.com/tamil-nadu/they-tortured-her-we-kept-sending-her-back-chartered-accountant-killed-tn-over-dowry-66040

Q&A: Sarthak Ahuja and Aditi Randev

Power couple **Sarthak Ahuja** and **Aditi Randev** are partners in life and business. Sarthak is an investment banker with over a decade of experience in startup advisory, and a Gold Medalist from the Indian School of Business. He is also the bestselling author of *Daily Coffee & Startup Fundraising*. He practices in areas of corporate finance, valuations, and transaction advisory, and educates entrepreneurs in these areas through his social media channels with a combined following of over 2.5 million. Aditi is a marketing and media professional. She has marketed music at Sony Music, cross-border commerce while at Meta, and currently heads the entire Media and Branding vertical at Niamh Ventures, an investment-banking firm across India and the Middle East.

1. Was discussing money always natural for both of you or did you have to develop a system for managing finances together?

S & A: Even during our courtship, we discussed how we liked to think about finances and managing them, and how it has been managed in our respective families to understand our individual relationship with money better. It's not just what you earn or spend, it's also about how you think about money that's important. As we work together in the same business, we happen to discuss it from a business and investments perspective often.

One of us tracks revenues and costs, while the other manages treasury and investments.

All personal spends are mostly in consultation with each other.

2. You both have strong professional identities. How do you balance individual career ambitions with domestic requirements? A lot of times couples find themselves unable to pursue their career dreams because of say, a home loan that needs the stability of a paycheck, or because they are the primary breadwinner. Another example would be having to work a certain kind of job because you're settling off family debt or are responsible getting your younger siblings settled. Not being able to talk about this with one's partner also ends up creating resentment between couples. It would be great if you could point out what young people need to talk about with their partners and how to work together to achieve mutual goals.

S & A: Within about a year of getting married, both of us thought of coming together to start a business. It was a tougher call for Aditi as she had to quit her job at Meta, and I was going to continue working in my family business so as to gradually phase into the new entity, which I could do over a year-and-a-half. But because we had conviction and belief in the idea—and in ourselves—we were able to take these calls.

Navigating the first year of entrepreneurship is tough because, for a business to take off, it takes a year of gestation and discovering Product-Market Fit. Thereafter, our identities and roles in the business became clearer, and now our business ventures fund our lifestyle and our savings for the future.

3. When it comes to sharing expenses, some couples split everything 50-50, some take individual heads and some merge finances completely. What approach has worked best for you, and why?

S & A: We have a joint account that pays our equal salaries from the business, and both of us have unrestricted access to the account for all expenses. It helps that our lifestyle ambitions are aligned.

4. Since being together, what's one financial lesson you've learned from each other that has shaped your approach to money?

S & A: Trust the other person with a responsibility and then get out of their way. Come in whenever they need you as a sounding board, but let them execute what they're responsible for.

5. If you had to give one piece of financial advice to couples—whether they're just dating, newly married, or managing a household together—what would it be?

S & A: Before you get married, speak openly about lifestyle ambitions because most resentments may be linked to what amount of financial independence gives someone peace of mind, and what level of lifestyle the other considers as the bare minimum. And these could be different levels and limits for different people. Once you're both aligned on what you're expecting out of your life—in terms of finances and what you'll be spending on—you'll have a clearer idea of financial compatibility.

7

Oh, Baby

I found out that I was pregnant 2 days before my husband and I were supposed to board a flight to Paris for a holiday.

I received the news in waves. At first, there was only shock and surprise—after all, we had only just started talking about having children, how could it happen so quickly?! This was followed by mild annoyance, for all my daydreams of walking along the streets of Paris sampling wine and cheese were now dashed. Finally, 4 days into our holiday and fuelled by the sugar from all the dessert I had been having during my trip, I felt gratitude. We were going to have a baby! Would she look like me? Would she be sporty or would she be artsy? Would she like to read? What would her favourite colour be? My baby at the time may have been just a bunch of cells glued together, but I had already begun dreaming about all the things she could be and all the things she would be.

Ten months later, on the day I gave birth, I learned two things—the first was that the girl I had been dreaming about was actually a boy. The second and more important takeaway was that from the day they're born, no, conceived, to the day that they get a job (and maybe even after), babies are expensive.

Are You Ready for a Baby?

In India, babies are considered to be among the most natural things that could happen in a woman's life, an inevitability even. School is followed by college. Vada pavs are followed by antacids. Marriage is followed by a baby. And then, another baby. The familial pressure on married couples to procreate is constant, and it's only fuelled by a culture that shows no restraint when it comes to commenting on the lives of others (it is considered representative of a person's perceived closeness to you). My husband and I took 3 years of marriage, of which 2 were spent smiling awkwardly at relatives who wanted to know when we were going to give them 'good news', to decide if and when we wanted kids, because we wanted to be sure that we were ready: mentally, physically, and financially.

The importance of financial 'readiness' in the context of having children cannot be stressed upon enough. You simply cannot have a baby if you don't have an assured and steady stream of income, apart from emergency savings to cover for all the costs that come along with your freshly minted little human. So how much does it cost to have and raise a baby in India? I've done the math. Before you go further, I'd recommend you fix yourself a strong drink, because you're going to need it by the time we're done.

Getting over the Bump—Pregnancy and Maternity Expenses

Getting pregnant is the easy part! Or so they say. As more people push the decision of having a child to their mid-and-late 30s because they want to get their career sorted, or haven't yet found the right person, or just don't want to have a baby in their 20s, the process of getting pregnant has become more complicated. While most couples and women in their 20s get pregnant with relative ease, older couples are increasingly seeking help by way of infertility treatments and In-Vitro-Fertilisation (IVF) procedures that are as expensive as they are exhausting.

The cost of IVF varies from city to city in India, but on average, it works out to anywhere between ₹1.5 lakh to ₹2.5 lakh, per cycle. This cost is exclusive of the additional blood tests and medicines that the couple might have to take. It's also important to note that the success rates of IVF vary with age. If you're under the age of 32, the chances of your getting pregnant with 1 round of IVF is 39%. If you're above 39 years of age, then you might require up to 5 rounds of IVF. So if you're thinking about postponing the baby decision for whatever reason, remember that delays can cost you, like literally. Your decision, therefore, is as much financial as it is emotional.

Pregnancy

Once you're pregnant (congratulations!), you need to find yourself a trustworthy Obstetrician-Gynaecologist (OBGYN) who, preferably, comes recommended by friends and family that have consulted him/her before. You also need to ensure that the hospital to which they belong suits your preferences. Would you rather give birth in a low-key nursing home that's close to your house? Or do you prefer the swanky specialty hospitals that come with maternity 'suites' and coffee shops? Specialty hospitals take an upfront payment of ₹1 lakh (and upwards) the moment you sign up with them. This money will be utilised as an advance that will be set off against doctor visits, scans, tests, labour, and room charges. Smaller nursing homes—which are still popular in India—take consultation fees for every visit and charge for tests and room charges etc. as and when they happen. If you end up having a C-Section for whatever reason, you will spend more by way of surgeon fees, Operating Theatre charges, and the like. Be prepared to spend at least ₹1 lakh during the course of your pregnancy.

Medical expenses aside, pregnancy also involves spending money on maternity clothes, prenatal exercise classes, shoes, underwear, and creams and oils for your growing belly.

Do You Need a Nanny?

When people tell you that it takes a village to raise a child, they aren't kidding. Children, especially babies and toddlers, require round the clock attention from adults around them and this can get extremely frustrating (and exhausting) if you're also trying to take care of the household or are working. The early days of a baby are also very challenging for couples because babies sleep very erratically and need to be fed at regular intervals. Midnight diaper changes, bottle cleaning, and breastfeeding can take a toll on you if you're attempting it alone. In India, a lot of new mothers choose to spend the first few months of the baby's life at their mother's house. However, if you aren't going to, for whatever reason, you might consider getting yourself a nanny. Be warned though—nannies, especially those who have been vetted and background checked, are expensive. A full-time nanny should cost you around ₹10,000 per month, depending on the city you live in.

When the Stork Arrives

The magnitude of the baby's expensiveness only dawns on you when they arrive. You'll find yourself scrolling down Amazon, bleary-eyed and sleepless, purchasing baby items that you weren't even aware existed. Sterilisers, bottles, breast pumps, cloth nappies, muslins, diapers, toys, mosquito nets, prams, car seats, diaper bags, rash creams, all the cute baby clothes that you can set your eyes on…the list is never ending. It's easy to get overwhelmed at this stage—after all, it's your baby we're talking about! But, even if you aren't the sort to get overwhelmed, expect to spend an average of ₹1 lakh during the first year of your baby's life on baby items and baby gear. You can save some costs by going the preloved route or actively asking for hand-me-downs from cousins and friends who've had children.

Insta-Baby

Are you also tempted by the 'bump to baby' photoshoots that flood your social media timelines every time a friend of yours gets pregnant? Does the idea of organising a baby shower excite you? Each of these very memorable events will set you back by ₹50,000, minimum. Neither of these things are necessary, by the way, even though there is a lot of peer pressure today to do them. Having said that, beautiful photos make wonderful memories and hanging out with loved ones will definitely bring you joy. If you can only choose one, go for the photoshoot because the photographs that you will receive at the end are truly precious.

Doing the Math

Here's a very rough estimate of the money you'll spend from pregnancy to the end of Year 1. If some items don't

Item	Average Cost in 2024 (₹)
IVF (1 Round)	2,00,000
Pregnancy Expenses (prenatal vitamins, personal care items, maternity clothes)	50,000
Tier 1 City Hospital Charges	1,50,000
Vaccinations in Year 1	50,000
Baby Gear (Car seat, pram, buggy, clothes, lotions, toys, diapers)	1,00,000
Baby Photoshoot/Shower	75,000
Nanny (from Month 6)	90,000
Total	**7,15,000**

apply to you, remove them to see how much you'll spend (on average) during the first year of your baby's life. You should have at least 50% of your estimated cost on hand when you start trying. If you don't, no worries! Just be sure to use a condom until you do.

Is Your Health Insurance Enough?

When you are planning for a baby, take a second look at your existing health insurance policy. Most health insurance plans in India do not cover the expenses of delivery (whether it's normal or via a C-Section surgery) and instead, include maternity coverage as an additional rider that you will have to pay extra premium for. Some plans even include new-born hospitalisation expenses and any medical charges that occur as a result of delivery complications.

Don't rush into upgrading your policy the moment you find out you're pregnant either—most plans have a waiting period of 24-48 months until the maternity benefit kicks in and no insurer will give you a maternity policy if you're already pregnant. So do your research! If you haven't got medical insurance and you're thinking about a baby, purchasing a policy with a maternity benefit should be at the top of your agenda. The extra premium is well worth the money.

Saving for Your Child's Education

Deciding on the school that your child will attend is one of the most, if not *the* most important decision you will make for him or her. You will have to sift through a number of subjective requirements before you zero in on the school that is best for your child and chief among those requirements is affordability. Schools can be expensive.

If you're in a metropolitan city, schooling will cost you in the upwards of ₹50,000 a year in tuition fees. There will also be lab fees, excursion fees, bus fees, and so on. Most schools also ask for one-time cash donations upright and these donations usually run into lakhs. This isn't applicable across all schools, of course, but it is something to be mindful of.

Bear in mind that this is only if you're opting for an Indian school board, like the CBSE or ICSE. Indian boards are regulated and there are measures in place to ensure that fees and fee increases aren't exorbitant.

However, if you're looking to admit your child in an international-board school, you're looking at a number that starts at around ₹3 lakh and goes up to ₹10 lakh for just tuition. I've plenty of acquaintances who are currently shelling ₹5+ lakh for elementary education because they're sure that their child will be going abroad for their undergraduation and of course, because they 'liked the crowd'.

The 'crowd' is a factor that younger, hipper parents go out of their way to vet when they look at schools. Will 'the crowd' at school be similar to them and their children? Will the parents of the other children be as educated as they are? As well-heeled?

The reason I want to pick apart this particular aspect is because the bulk of invisible (but significant) spending that happens while your child is at school is because of peer pressure. The Pokemon, cricket, and WWE trading cards, the Pentium III PCs, and the Nokia 6600s of the 90s and early-2000s have now mutated into X-Boxes, PlayStations, iPads, smartphones, and laptops.

Birthday parties are bigger than ever, with parents going all out with themes and 5-star venues. If you can afford this lifestyle (and you're still reading this book, thank you!), there is no problem. The problem begins when you send your child to a school with parents and students in an income and societal bracket that is aspirational.

Add this to the fact that kids are incredibly observant and sensitive to the things that are around them, and well, you need to be ready with one of two things—the ability to convince a child that hedonism is pointless and that material goods only give you false security, or money.

Here's an estimate, on the opposite page, of how much you'll spend on your child's schooling (assuming your child goes to the average Metropolitan CBSE school):

The good news is that your child's education is staggered, which means that except for the donation, you don't require the entire sum outright. But you will require a surplus of ₹1,00,000 every year to cover your child's school expenses.

Item	Cost in ₹
One Time Donation	2,50,000
Tuition Fees (KG to Class XII)	10,00,000
Extra curricular classes	4,80,000
Special Exams & tests	1,00,000
School & Project Related Expenses	1,50,000
Miscellaneous Fees	1,20,000
Total	**21,00,000**

The Truth about Child Endowment Plans

A Child Endowment Plan is an insurance-investment hybrid that many banks and insurance agents sell aggressively to new parents as the best investment they can make for their children. Parents will pay a sum of money every month as a premium for a specified period and once the policy period comes to an end, they will receive a lump-sum amount. If the parent passes away before the policy period is completed, the child will receive an assured sum of money when they come of age and the premium amount will no longer be required to be paid.

Child plans are sold by bank relationship managers and insurance agents the moment they get a whiff of childbirth in the family. You'll hear terms like 'securing your child's future' and 'tax savings' and 'funding higher education' being thrown around.

While tax savings (the premiums are tax-deductible and the sum received on maturity is tax-free) is certainly true, you're more likely to receive better post-tax returns by investing in equity mutual funds.

Often times, child plans are also purchased without really paying attention to whether the final amount will be enough for your child's needs after taking into account the price rise that has occurred over the years.

My parents bought a child plan for me in the year 1992, where they were told that they had to pay something around ₹30,000 over the course of 10 years (₹3,000 a year) and they would receive Rs 1 lakh in 2012, which they could use for my higher education. ₹1 lakh may have been a princely sum in 1992, but in 2012? Not really.

But if it sucks as an investment, why are people so keen on selling it? *Commissions.* These products come with benefits (that are likely greater) for the seller of the policy than the one who's actually investing. So there is more motivation, and hence they're sold more aggressively by relationship managers and agents. This is especially prevalent during the early days of the child's birth when parents are emotionally vulnerable and overwhelmed with what's going on in their life.

While it's important to have a basket of investments for your child's future, the endowment plans, with their predatory selling and mediocre returns, are best avoided.

Customise Your Savings According to Your Child

Your child is unique and, therefore, her needs will be unique. Take some time to think about what your child will require in the short, medium, and long term and plot your investments accordingly. Does your child have a medical issue that might require special attention in the future? Does she play a sport that might require (expensive) professional coaching soon? Save independently for each of these needs, apart from setting aside money for an emergency fund that can help cover sudden and unexpected expenses.

Saving for Daughters—the Sukanya Samriddhi Scheme

If you've been blessed with a daughter, or just have a baby girl in your life, the Sukanya Samriddhi Scheme is actually a fantastic option to build out a nest-egg for her.

The Sukanya Samriddhi Yojana (SSY) is a government-backed savings scheme launched under the Beti Bachao, Beti Padhao campaign. The goal of the scheme is to provide incentives to parents to save for their daughters in a way that is simple and effective.

Here's How It Works

- ⇨ Every girl child gets to have one (and only one) SSY account, which can be opened at Post Offices across India.
- ⇨ You can save up to ₹1.5 lakh a year under this scheme. This contribution you make is *tax deductible under section 80C.*

⇨ Your contribution earns interest every year. The interest rates on average have been in the whereabouts of 8%, making it much higher than any regular FD.

⇨ You need to make this contribution for 15 years. And after 21 years, the account matures, and the funds are released. This amount is totally tax free!

PERIOD	RATE OF INTEREST (%)
01.10.2016 TO 31.03.2017	8.5
01.04.2017 TO 30.06.2017	8.4
01.07.2017 TO 31.12.2017	8.3
01.01.2018 TO 30.09.2018	8.1
01.10.2018 TO 30.06.2019	8.5
01.07.2019 TO 31.03.2020	8.4
01.04.2020 TO 31.03.2023	7.6
01.04.2023 TO 31.12.2023	8.0
01.01.2024 TO 31.03.2025	8.2

Sukanya Samriddhi Scheme Interest Rates.
Source: National Savings Institute,
Ministry of Finance (DEA) Govt of India

So, if you invested ₹1.5 lakh a year under this scheme, you'd have

1. Invested ₹22,50,000 (1,50,000 x 15), and
2. You'd receive around ₹1,02,56,046 after 21 years! What's more, this amount is tax free.

Is There a Catch?

There is a lack of liquidity in this scheme. The investment is locked until the child turns 18, after which only partial withdrawals (up to 50%) are allowed. What's more, these withdrawals are allowed only if it's in the case of the girl's wedding or higher education. So even if she was facing a medical emergency, withdrawal won't be allowed.

There is also an age limit. You can only open an SSY account for your child if she's under the age of 10.

Finally, the scheme is restricted to 2 daughters per family. If you had twins/triplets after you had your first daughter, then there's an exception (but not the other way around).

But despite the minor quibbles, the Sukanya Samriddhi Scheme is a fail-safe—and tax efficient—way to build a nest egg for your daughter. I'd highly recommend this scheme for parents of girl children, especially if your daughter(s) is under the age of 5. It is certainly much more meaningful than the expensive 'child plans' that claim to combine insurance and investment but end up providing neither.

The Cost of Your Career

I returned to work after close to 7 months of maternity leave. The transition was easy for me since I worked in my father's practice. I had the flexibility to leave early if I wanted to, I could work from home, and most importantly, I had a supportive family setup so I could leave my baby with my parents or my in-laws while I was at work. I also got a nanny who came in during the day. Even with this entire village behind me, I had days where I wanted to give up because the guilt of leaving my baby at home became overwhelming.

Bright young women with fancy degrees dropping out of the workforce is something I am accustomed to seeing, for it keeps happening even in my family. Two of my cousins who are chartered accountants, quit their respective jobs when they had their first child. Another cousin, who was on track for a senior management role at Goldman Sachs, also quit her job after she delivered her daughter. None of them were happy about it, but they've all made their peace with it. After all, they were the primary caregivers for their children.

Indra Nooyi, the CEO of PepsiCo, famously remarked that a woman's Biological Clock was constantly in conflict with her Career Clock. It's a struggle for new mothers to return to the workforce, especially in India where you have to juggle societal expectations along with guilt and hormones and work-related pressure. So it's really no surprise then, that according to a survey conducted by the Associated Chamber of Commerce (Assocham), a whopping 25% of first time Indian mothers quit their jobs after they had a baby.[1]

It's easy to see why. The lack of women in the workforce has ensured that offices are as baby unfriendly as they've ever been. Moms can't bring their baby to work. If you're a young mother who's breastfeeding, finding a clean, private space to pump is next to impossible. Your work hours aren't as flexible as they used to be either—you'll have to be home at a certain time and on some days, even cut your day short. Post-office plans and impromptu drinks with your colleagues are also things you may have to temporarily forget about. Being a young working mother is hard.

And the pandemic—followed by organisations that are now insisting on 'returning to the office'—has made it worse. McKinsey had predicted that 1 in 4 women were considering downshifting their careers or leaving the workforce entirely because of COVID-19.[2] Although the lockdowns forced men across the world to be aware of all the invisible challenges that women took on every day as they managed home and work, structural changes will take time. And until that happens, understandably, mothers will continue to quit the workforce.

While the decision to quit your job after a baby is entirely yours, I want to draw your attention to two things. The first is that during the first week of March 2017, the Indian Parliament approved a bill that raised paid maternity leave for new mothers from 12 weeks/3 months to 26 weeks/6 months. This increase propelled India to the third place in the list of countries with the highest-paid maternity leave (following Norway and Canada). The move was geared to increase the retention of women in the workforce, given that our country ranks very poorly when it comes to female labour force participation. If you are planning for a baby, remember that you have 6 months of paid maternity leave. Take full advantage of it.

The second is that if you're indeed going to quit your job after having a baby, you need to start hoarding and saving aggressively at least a year before you quit. The loss of your own, independent stream of income will be difficult to cope with if you don't. If you want to work, but can't leave the baby, research options for freelancing and don't be afraid to ask for opportunities.

The truth is that women cannot have it all. We are playing a game we simply cannot win, but that isn't to say that we ought to stop playing. The income that you earn post a baby, whether it's from your job or from freelancing, will most certainly be of help when it comes to raising your child. After all, it's only when you become a parent do you realise that money is entirely capable of buying happiness.

Oh, Baby—The TL; DR

Is Your Bank Account Ready for a Baby?

In India, having a child is often treated as an inevitability, but the decision is as financial as it is emotional. You need a steady income and emergency savings before expanding your family.

Pregnancy and Maternity Costs

IVF treatments can cost ₹1-2.5 lakh per cycle, with lower success rates as you age. Specialty hospitals charge upwards of ₹1 lakh in advance for maternity services. Add in prenatal vitamins, baby gear, maternity clothes, and vaccinations—expect your expenses to hit all-time highs!

Double Check Your Health Insurance

Most health insurance policies in India don't cover maternity expenses unless you've added a rider—and there's usually a 24–48 month waiting period. Plan ahead and upgrade your policy well in advance if needed.

We Don't Need No Education Expenses

A CBSE or ICSE education in a metro city costs ₹50,000+ per year for tuition alone, not counting donations and extra-curricular activities. International schools can cost ₹3-10 lakhs annually.

Peer pressure in elite schools can lead to unexpected expenses—think gadgets, premium birthday parties, and fancy field trips.

Don't Fall for the Child Plans

Endowment plans marketed as 'child plans' often offer mediocre returns compared to mutual funds. Keep insurance and investment separate!

Can Moms Have It All?

Many women in India leave the workforce after having children—25% of first-time mothers quit their jobs. Maternity leave now extends to 6 months, but if you plan to quit, start saving aggressively at least a year in advance to offset the loss of income.

Notes

1. TNN, '25% of first time moms quit jobs for their kids', *The Times of India*, 10 May 2015. https://timesofindia.indiatimes.com/india/25-first-time-moms-quit-jobs-for-their-kids/articleshow/47219383.cms
2. Justine Jablonska (ed.), 'Seven charts that show COVID-19's impact on women's employment', *McKinsey & Company*, 8 March 2021. https://www.mckinsey.com/featured-insights/diversity-and-inclusion/seven-charts-that-show-covid-19s-impact-on-womens-employment

8

Is Borrowing in Your Interest?

Almost House Owners

In late 2019, my husband and I *almost* bought a house. We saw the property, we liked it enough, we knew it was expensive (the EMI would eat most of our combined pay checks, and we'd just had a child) but were also pushed by the notion that this was what people did in their 30s. We applied for the loan, got approved...and the week before we had to send the down payment, chickened out.

The experience of telling the sellers (and apologising profusely) was incredibly embarrassing. 30-somethings these days! And while we cringed through the back-pedalling we had to do with the bankers and all the other parties involved, we knew we'd taken the right decision. Maybe we could've afforded that house on paper, but not in real life. To do the right thing (be cautious about your finances) by not doing the *right thing* (increasing your assets) was a weird feeling.

4 months later, the pandemic hit. As did sweet, sweet EMI-free relief.

Loans Are good, Loans Are Bad

Loans are like rocket fuel—in that they can propel you towards big goals like an educational degree, buying a home, or starting your entrepreneurship journey. But just like rocket fuel, it can explode, leaving behind damage that can take years to correct.

The good news is that you don't need a physics degree to work this out.

What's Your Score?

If you've ever read personal finance books and other related literature like columns, blogs, or even podcasts by western authors, especially those from the United States and United Kingdom, you'd know that the Credit Score is incredibly important in the west if you want to have a positive relationship with your banker. While the west is more evolved in terms of credit, India is now fast catching up.

A 2023 report from *Paisabazaar* reveals that 64% of consumers acquired their first credit product (loans or credit cards) before they turned 30. And among these, a significant 37% were under the age of 25.[1] As more and more young Indians become credit aware, the need for a solid credit score is greater than ever.

What Are Credit Scores?

A Credit Score, or a Credit Rating, is a 3-digit number between 300 to 900 that is allocated to you based on your borrowing habits. Think of it as marks that you receive from your banks and financial institutions for your performance in the subject of financial discipline. A good credit score is above 700. 800+ and you're a class topper.

This score is calculated based on a number of factors, including how regular you are with paying your credit card bills on time, your loan repayment history, how long you've maintained lines of credit (loans and cards) and whether or not a bank has had to move to court to recover loans from you. The higher your credit score, the more desirable you are to the bank as a potential lender.

How Does It Work?

Your Credit Score is calculated by Credit Information Bureaus. There are currently 4 such bureaus in India—TransUnion CIBIL, Equifax, Experian, and High Mark.

Every time you make a transaction that impacts your credit card (for example, paying your credit card bill or an EMI), this information is submitted by your bank to these credit information companies. This sending of information is mandated by the RBI. Today, fintechs even have access to information about your rent and utility payments.

Every time you sign up for a credit card or take on an EMI, you're agreeing to this in the fine print. With our phones linked to our PAN cards linked to our Aadhar cards linked to whatever app we're using to make our payments, collecting information about these transactions has become easier than ever.

These credit bureaus then collate the information and arrive at a score based on your transactions. The methodology of arriving at the credit score by all 4 bureaus is extremely similar, so if you have a poor score with one bureau, it's highly unlikely that it will be better with another.

How Do I Get a Good Score?

If you already have a credit card or have taken a loan, making regular payments in full and on time will bump up your score. These days, credit scores are taken into consideration by banks for all kinds of loans, so having a good score will play a part in your getting the loan, especially when you don't have any kind of previous/family relationship with your bank. If you've never taken any line of credit before, your score will be neutral (neither good nor bad).

If you want to improve your credit score, consider getting a basic credit card (you'll get a free card with your savings bank account). Use it to make small but regular payments—think streaming subscriptions and monthly groceries. Pay off your balance in full each month. And avoid late payments like the plague—delays can knock points off your score faster than you can say 'minimum due'.

Tracking Helps!

A TransUnion CIBIL report stated in 2024 that consumers who actively track and monitor their credit, have higher scores—ranging around 729. Those who didn't monitor, weren't far behind at 712. Having said that, the report also states that 46% of those who engage in self-monitoring saw their scores increase in 6 months. Credit-score tracking, that way, is very similar to calorie counting. Once you get up and close with it and find ways to fix it, improvement is inevitable. This isn't just for folks in the 729 category.

If you've got a lower score, give yourself a year of tracking (and regular repayments)—you'll see it back on the rise.

Why Your Score Matters

Availing a line of credit can be potentially life-saving during emergencies, especially for women, who might not always have solid securities or assets that they can pledge in a moment's notice. However, the disbursement of these loans are dependent on the individual's credit score, which is why it is important for women to not only be aware of their credit scores, but also work towards making them a number to be proud of.

Vocabulary Class—Loan Edition

Loans come with their own vocabulary. Here's what you should know before you come anywhere close to taking one.

- ⇨ **Principal:** The original amount of money that you're borrowing.
- ⇨ **Interest:** The money you pay the bank for borrowing the money, calculated as a percentage of the principal.
- ⇨ **Tenure:** How long you're going to take to repay the loan. The thumb rule is that the longer the tenure, the lower the interest rate. Why? Because

banks get to collect more interest from you over the years. The shorter the tenure, the higher the interest rate. That's why personal loans charge 14-18% interest per annum, while home loans are in the whereabouts of 8-10%. Credit cards charge a cool 24-36% interest per annum.

- **EMI (Equated Monthly Installment):** The monthly amount you pay back to the lender. It's part principal, part interest. During the initial years of borrowing, the ratio of principal and interest in the EMI will heavily skew towards interest. So during your initial years of repayment, remember that you're mostly just paying off interest. It is only in the middle and towards the end of your loan that your principal gets repaid. Why is this important? Because if you delay repayments, or miss them, the bank gets to charge fresh interest on the remaining portion of your principal.
- **Floating Interest Rate:** For some loans, you can choose to take a floating interest rate, where the interest rate changes based on market trends. It's a gamble—because there's no telling if interest rates will go down or shoot up.
- **Fixed Interest Rate:** Predictable and stable rate of interest.
- **Collateral:** An asset that you can give to the lender as security. When you take a home loan, the house itself is a collateral. The bank is essentially saying, yes, we'll help you buy the house, but if you stop paying us back, the house becomes ours.

To Borrow or Not to Borrow

At an age when anything and everything can be paid via EMIs, explaining the 'types of loans' feels moot. Instead, I'd rather share a blanket set of rules that you can follow *no matter what* you're looking to borrow for.

1. *50% Cap on EMIs*

Your total EMIs—home, personal, car, combined—shouldn't exceed 50% of household income. Imagine having less than half a pay check for your regular expenses! There could be a serious stress on your finances if it exceeds this limit.

2. *Basics before Borrowing*

Get your emergency fund and your insurance documents in place before you borrow. If you're taking a large loan, make sure you have term insurance for the amount so *if*, in the remote chance that something happens to you, your dependents aren't burdened with its repayment.

3. *Borrow for What You Already Have*

Here's a little secret from the finances of the wealthy—they take loans despite having the means to buy outright. Why? Because the money parked in their investments grows at a greater rate than the loan interest.

Their mutual fund investments will grow in double digits while bank loans would be in single digits. So they end up making a marginal amount of money by borrowing.

Now here's what I want you to take away—the wealthy

only borrow for what they *already* have. You only need to pay a 20% down payment, but saving up to 40-50% of the property's value can go a long way in boosting your confidence when it comes to repayment. You wouldn't have wiped out your savings, and you'd still have a buffer for other needs.

Remember, this is not a strategy that works for everyone. Some prefer the peace of mind that comes with paying off a significant loan versus waiting on arbitrage.

4. *Don't Borrow for Discretion*

A lending boom, low financial awareness, lower household savings, and a lot of ambition among India's young people comes together to form a terrible cocktail of debt. FREED, an Indian debt resolution platform, states that a third of millennials and 40% of Gen-Z are currently dealing with 'unsustainable borrowings'. The average FREED client, they report has an average of 6 loans totalling up to ₹5,60,000. These loans are often taken out for discretionary needs—like phones, concert tickets, and travel to name a few.

The lure of EMIs is undeniable. A basic Marshall speaker, which costs around Rs 15,000, suddenly becomes that much more appealing when it's shown to be priced at Rs 2,500 for 6 months. An iPhone works out to Rs 15,000 for 6 months. That's not bad at all, you say, and check out. Designer jeans are no longer out of reach at Rs 1,500 for 6 months. And just like that, you've got a beautiful speaker, the latest phone, and designer jeans at Rs 19,000. The instant gratification feels powerful. It feels like you can buy anything.

The problem is, not only is discretionary borrowing a terrible financial habit, it's an incredibly expensive one. If you're not paying attention, interest rates can go up to 48% per annum, not to mention the mounting stress and pressure that can come with debt that piles on.

So don't borrow for things or experiences that you want but can't fully afford just yet. Saving and paying in full is well worth the trouble—and feels so much better!

5. *Cars Depreciate*

A car is a depreciating asset. It loses value over time. If you're looking to borrow to get your dream car, make sure you have at least 40% of the car's value paid out. Your loan shouldn't exceed 4 years and the EMI shouldn't cross 10% of your monthly pay. No car is worth more effort—and if it is, you probably shouldn't be buying it.

6. *Don't Buy the Circus for a Monkey*

When you take on a large loan, especially the likes of a home loan or a large business loan, the banks might try and pressurise you to buy additional products, like term life insurance. While having term life insurance is necessary when you're taking on a large loan, you're not legally bound to buy from the bank, or even have term life insurance in the first place. Don't fall for these tactics or the pressure from bank staff to make you buy products you don't need.

7. *BONUS: Never Borrow to Invest*

Never, ever, borrow to invest. Don't take my word for it—Warren Buffet, the world's most successful investor, said in his 1991 commencement speech in Notre Dame University, 'I've seen more people fail because of liquor and leverage—leverage being borrowed money.' Buffett warned investors to avoid putting borrowed money in any sort of equities. And I would go out on a limb to say that he knows more about investing than the rest of us do.

Loans are what you take to bridge *needs* and in case of *emergencies*. Trying your hand at options trading (which isn't too different from playing poker at Vegas if you're not technically qualified to), is neither a need nor an emergency. And it can land you in very deep, and very dark waters.

Investments should be made only with your own money.

Pay Off or Invest?

This is an important debate to have—especially if you have multiple loans. Here's a framework you can use to make the decision:

1. *PAY OFF: High-Interest Loans*

High-interest loans, like credit-card debt or personal loans with rates above 18-20%, should be cleared as soon as possible. These loans accumulate interest at a pace far greater than any investment, making them financial quicksand.

2. *INVEST: Long-Term Loans*

Loans such as home loans or education loans that come with lower interest rates (7-8%) can be paid off as scheduled while you focus on growing your investments. Since these loans often offer tax benefits, they can work to your advantage if managed wisely.

3. *PAY OFF: If You Hate Debt*

Some of us are more comfortable with debt than others. If the idea of EMIs gnaw at you, try paying off your shorter loans before their tenure. You can also look to foreclose your larger loans, *provided* you're investing the bare minimum on the side. Sometimes the winds can get strong, and you don't want to be caught naked.

4. *PAY OFF AND INVEST: If You Receive an Inheritance or a Windfall*

If you receive a financial windfall, look to clear all or at least a significant portion of your debt, while making sure you have a portion left for bumping up your investments. If you're conservative, allocate 90% of your windfall towards debt and 10% towards investing. If you're more on the moderate side of the risk-o-meter, you can invest up to 30% of your windfall.

Loans Are a Bridge, Not a Trap Door

Loans can be powerful allies in building your future—but only if you play by the rules. Maintain a strong credit score, decode the jargon, avoid overshooting your budget, and focus on clearing high-interest loans before dreaming of investments.

Is Borrowing in Your Interest?—The TL; DR

Loans Are Rocket Fuel

Loans can help you level up in life—whether it's getting that degree, buying a home, or starting a business. But like rocket fuel, if mishandled, they can blow up your finances.

Credit Scores 101

Think of your credit score (300–900) as your financial GPA. A score above 700? Gold star. Over 800? Class topper! What affects it? Paying your bills on time, how much credit you've taken, and your repayment history. Pay off your credit card in full each month—don't just scrape by with the 'minimum due'.

The Rules of Borrowing Club

- ⇨ **50% EMI Cap:** Your EMIs shouldn't take more than half your household income—anything more, and you're heading for a financial nightmare.
- ⇨ **Safety First:** Build your emergency fund and sort your insurance before taking on a big loan.
- ⇨ **Borrow with a Backup:** Ideally, save 40-50% of the asset's value before taking a loan—it'll make repayments so much less stressful.
- ⇨ **Skip Loans for Splurges:** EMIs for gadgets, designer clothes, or holidays may seem harmless, but they can trap you in high-interest debt.

The EMI Trap

Breaking down a big expense into ₹2,500 EMIs makes it feel affordable, right? But those tiny EMIs can snowball into a mountain of debt, with interest rates climbing up to 48% annually.

Never Borrow to Invest

Even Warren Buffett says borrowing money to invest is a terrible idea. No stock or hot new asset class is worth risking a loan. Investments should come from your savings—not borrowed cash.

Loans Can Be a Lifeline

Loans can be your lifeline or your downfall—it all comes down to how you use them. Keep your credit score strong, understand what you're signing up for, and stay on top of high-interest debts before you start chasing new investments.

Notes

1. 'Making India Credit Fit', Volume 3.0, *Paisabazaar*, November 2023. https://static.paisabazaar.com/media/web/credit_fit_volume.pdf

9

What Does Retirement Look Like?

Planning for Your Career's Sundowner

I've a confession to make. I've been dreaming about retiring ever since I joined the workforce 17 years ago. For those of us running the seemingly never-ending rat race, retirement feels like an indulgent fantasy—a time when you can actually just put your feet up on the sofa, read for as long as you like, finally tend to your plants, and never have to 'circle back' for anything. A life without Powerpoint and Excel!

Retirement today looks very different from what it did for our parents' generation. For starters, they didn't work the hours we did, nor did they carry the same amount of stress. India is one of the top overworked countries globally. According to the latest data from the International Labour Organization (ILO), the average Indian worker clocks 46.7 hours each week and 51% of the Indian workforce works more than 49 hours a week.[1] Another survey by McKinsey states Indians report the highest workplace burnout symptoms, with 59% of employees stating they are experiencing some form of burnout or the other. Indian employees also reported the highest levels of workplace exhaustion at 62%.[2]

Little wonder then, that everyone's trying to 'retire' as soon as they can.

This Girl Is on FIRE (Financial Independence, Retire Early)

There has been a substantial increase in interest in the FIRE movement in India among the 40 and below age group. FIRE, which stands for Financial Independence, Retire Early, proposes that young people stay frugal, save aggressively, and invest smartly so they can quit the rat race early to live their best lives. Instead of saving for your retirement over a 30-40-year career period, you save for it over a 10-15-year period.

In theory, it sounds doable, but in practicality, FIRE can burn you out quicker than a demanding workplace. A large part of FIRE-ing is giving up on mainstream lifestyle choices. Skipping post-work cocktails is one thing, but would you be ready to not date, not travel, or not have children? Would you be willing to postpone your dream vacation to Europe to your 50s? Would you be okay with putting your child in a second-tier school because the first-tier ones are too expensive?

FIRE deals with a type of extreme behaviour that is more beneficial to those who already have an existing cushion—in terms of wealth, and in terms of networks.

FIRE, in many ways, is an outlet for young professionals

who're more or less sick of the stress that Indian workplaces bring. It is an escape hatch from being employed, because who in their right minds would do this for 40 years?! They're not to be blamed though. There is an urgent need to fix the burnout in Indian workplaces, a fix that might just need higher-order intervention.

In the meantime, regular retirement planning isn't getting the spotlight it deserves. We're living longer than ever—meaning, retirement could last as long as your career, or longer. This longevity comes with greater medical needs and a higher cost of living, so saving for your retirement requires more thought today than ever before.

How Much Money Do You Need for Retirement?

You can't save effectively until you know how much you'll need. And what do you need? A standard rule is to aim for 30 times your annual expenses at the time of retirement. So if you spend ₹12 lakh per annum today, you'd need ₹3.6 crores for retirement.

While that's a good starting point, I believe that this number doesn't do justice to the complexities that life throws at us. Here's what I want you to *also* think about and ask yourself:

- ⇨ How old do I want to be when I'm retired?
- ⇨ How many years away is it?
- ⇨ What do I see myself doing?
- ⇨ What does a typical day look like?
- ⇨ What is my family's life stage at this point?

- ⇨ What would my partner's needs be? Would they be dependent on me? What does their career look like?
- ⇨ Who else would still be dependent on me? Will I still be caring for my parents at this point?
- ⇨ What would my children's needs be?

Answering all these questions will help you get closer to the number that you'll need year on year.

Don't Forget Inflation

Inflation hits you 2 ways when you're saving for retirement. The first is the inflation during your career and earning time, where it eats into your ability to save because of higher prices. The second is when it reduces the value of your savings over a long period of time. So when you're saving for a longer horizon, you need to save an amount that's larger than you anticipated.

I'll spare you the formulae—today, technology has bestowed a number of handy 'retirement planning' calculators that are a simple google search away (I personally like the ClearTax and the Prime Investor retirement calculator[3]). All you have to do is put in your age, when you expect to retire, and what you estimate your monthly expenses to be, and it'll draw up the number for you.

Tree or Basket?

There are 2 ways you can look at your retirement corpus. The first way is to see it as a large nest egg that will generate returns after which you can pass it on to your child/children, like a tree. The tree continues to stay on, provided it's well-tended by your children and dependents, and allows them to enjoy its fruits as well.

The other way to look at your retirement corpus is to save a sum of money that you can keep withdrawing from. It could earn some basic interest over time, but like a fruit basket, it will get empty, and you can't guarantee that your dependents will have anything left.

There's no perfect approach. If you're a DINK (Double Income, No Kids) couple who want to stay childless, for example, you're better off thinking about the basket. If you've kids, on the other hand, you might want to think about investing in something that your children can also enjoy.

Provident Funds and National Pension Scheme

We can't talk about retirement without talking about India's marquee retirement schemes—the Provident Fund (PF) and the National Pension Scheme. Here's what you need to know:

What and How: PF

Provident funds are governed by The Employees' Provident Fund and Miscellaneous Provisions Act, 1952. If you work in any organisation with 20 or more employees, your company is required to register with the Employee Provident Fund Organization (EPFO) and deduct provident fund contributions from your salary. (For smaller organisations, it's optional, but most progressive workplaces do it.)

Provident Fund has two parts:

- ⇨ Your contribution—deducted from your salary.
- ⇨ Your employer's contribution—added by your company.

Both of these go into your EPF (Employees' Provident Fund) account, where they earn interest. In FY 2022-23, that interest rate was 8.15%—not as high as 2016-17's 8.65%, but still miles better than what your savings account gives you.

Your contribution is 12% of your basic pay (and dearness allowance, if at all it's a part of your salary). Your employer will match your contribution of 12%, so 24% of your basic salary goes towards the EPF scheme. What you need to know is that the scheme itself is split into:

1. The Employee Provident Fund Account: Your nest egg that earns interest. Your entire 12% contribution goes here, along with 3.67% of your employer's contribution.
2. The Employee Pension Scheme: This scheme will pay a pension to your children and spouse in case of an untimely death. 8.33% of your employer's contribution (up to ₹15,000) is paid towards the employee pension scheme. If your basic salary is above ₹15,000, the deduction over and above ₹15,000 is credited towards your Employee Provident Fund or nest egg account.

Provident fund is mandatory for all employees whose salary is below ₹15,000. For those earning above ₹15,000 per month, you can opt-in voluntarily. But keep in mind that your employer is only required to contribute 12% on ₹15,000 (i.e., ₹1,800/month), even if you choose to contribute more from your side.

A few generous companies match your higher contributions, but this depends on their policy, and let's be honest, your luck.

Wait, What about the New Tax Regime?

Here's the deal: If you've switched to the new income tax regime, contributions to PF no longer offer tax deductions under Section 80C. So, while the money is still being saved and earning interest, it won't reduce your taxable income the way it used to under the old regime.

That said:

- ⇨ The interest you've earned in your EPF account is still tax-free.
- ⇨ So is the payout at retirement.

So, PF continues to be a smart, low-risk savings tool—even if it's no longer a tax hack under the new rules.

Still in the old regime? Great—your contribution gets you a deduction under Section 80C, interest is tax-free, and the final amount you get at retirement is also exempt. Don't mistake the trees for the forest though. Unless you've significant deductions, the new regime is still the more favourable option for most up-and-coming salary earners.

Other Updates Worth Knowing

You now have a Universal Account Number (UAN) that stays with you even when you change jobs—no more opening a fresh PF account every time you jump ship. You can also do an e-nomination online (do it—it takes 5 minutes and will make life easier for your loved ones later).

Just don't expect a glamorous user interface. The EPFO website still looks like it was built by a guy who coded the HTML on his Windows 98 PC.

Pros: Attractive Even Without the Tax Deductions

PF continues to be an attractive option for earners across all wage ranges despite the more recent tax changes because it provides steady, reliable growth and tax-free returns at the time of maturity.

Cons: No Dipping

Perhaps the only downside to the provident fund is that it doesn't allow you to withdraw in full unless:

- ⇨ You've reached the ripe retirement age of 58 years, or,
- ⇨ You've been unemployed for more than 2 months (you'll need to do a self-declaration).

You can also withdraw your provident fund in part for a number of reasons, including your child's marriage, to fund a home purchase, to repay a home loan, or to pay for a medical emergency. Bear in mind that there are a number of conditions and requirements for each of these withdrawals. A provident fund's ability to give you a nest egg depends fully on how long you'll allow it to compound.

What and How: NPS

The National Pension Scheme (NPS) is a retirement-focused investment plan backed by the government. Think of it as provident fund's updated cousin who's into investing. A provident fund is a fairly straightforward savings scheme. NPS, on the other hand, lets you grow your money by investing in a mix of equity (stocks), corporate bonds, and government securities.

NPS also allows you to choose how aggressive or conservative you want to be. You can go for:

- ⇨ Equity (E): Expect higher returns but also market ups and downs.
- ⇨ Corporate Bonds (C): Stable but slightly more adventurous than government bonds.
- ⇨ Government Bonds (G): The 'grandparent-approved' option—safe and steady.

You Need to Know about Corporate NPS

While regular NPS is something you sign up for as an individual, corporate NPS is where your employer pitches in too, very similar to how PF works.

If you're a salaried employee and your company has registered for the Corporate NPS model with the Pension Fund Regulatory and Development Authority (PFRDA), you're eligible. It's optional for employers, which means not every company offers it—so you'll want to check in with your HR team and ask if they've signed up.

Why Corporate NPS Is a Game-changer

In a Corporate NPS setup, your employer contributes a portion of your salary—either 10% or 14% depending on the tax regime you're on—to your NPS account. So apart from your contribution, they're also pitching in towards your retirement. This is over and above your CTC in most cases, and here's the best part: **It's tax-deductible no matter which regime you're in.**

Let's break it down:

- ⇨ Under the old tax regime, a private company's employer could contribute up to 10% of the employee's basic salary.
- ⇨ But if you've switched to the new tax regime, then your employer can go up to 14%—just like government employees.
- ⇨ This part of your salary that has gone towards the NPS contribution is tax deductible under Section 80CCD(2) *under both regimes!*

It's quite evident that the government is promoting Corporate NPS aggressively, because in the clean deduction-free landscape of the new regime, Corporate NPS stands out like a lone banyan tree. The only point to note here is that the total employer contribution across NPS + PF can't exceed ₹7.5 lakh in a year. Anything above this gets taxed as a perquisite, as a part of your salary.

If you've just about started on your career, the corporate NPS offers you a powerful lever to save on taxes while saving for your future.

Pros: Way More Tax Efficient

Apart from being capable of shielding a significant portion of your income form tax, NPS can give you higher returns as well (historically around 10% in equity-heavy portfolios). And, in comparison to mutual funds, the fund management fees are peanuts.

So why isn't everyone putting their money in NPS? I'll tell you.

Cons: Lock-in and Annuities

Just like PFs, there are lock-ins. Once you invest, you can't just cash out whenever you want. You'll need to wait until you hit 60 to withdraw the full amount. And when you retire, you're required to use 40% of your NPS savings to buy an annuity (a plan that gives you a monthly pension). Let's say your payout is ₹1 crore. You mandatorily must put ₹40 lakh in an annuity scheme that pays you a monthly pension. The idea is that you're not spending your nest egg in one go, but making sure there's money left for you as you age. You have several options for the type of annuity you want to take, but this is mandatory. And this pension is subject to tax.

Which Is Better?

Although there was a point when the PF and NPS schemes were on equal footing, NPS has now raced ahead thanks to significant tax benefits and higher market-linked returns. The right answer to this question though, is that you need both. Building your retirement nest egg isn't the function or responsibility of one single type of investment.

Don't Fall for the Retirement Plan Ads, Please

I love the retirement plan ads that insurance companies push out on TV. Sentimental children who've set their parents up. Senior citizens skydiving, living their best lives. But that's more or less where my love ends. While the ads are excellent, the product is mediocre.

Retirement Annuity Insurance Schemes are insurance-investment plans offered by insurance companies that promise payouts after retirement.

They're pitched as plans with 'guaranteed returns' and offer a fixed payout for life, which *sounds* comforting. There may also be a life insurance component for your dependents.

The truth is that these plans offer only 4-6% annual returns, which barely keep up with inflation. Annuity plans also require larger investments, which means your money is tied up for years, and there's little-to-no flexibility for early withdrawals.

And finally, insurance-linked investments often come with hidden fees and agent commissions that eat into your returns.

I will repeat this as often as I have to: Separate your insurance and investment. Buy a term insurance policy for life cover and use mutual funds or provident fund/NPS for growth. Term insurance is cheaper and provides higher coverage without confusing you with 'returns'.

There's No One Way

The ideal retirement portfolio balances growth, safety, and liquidity. You can use a combination of mutual funds (especially equity) for long-term growth, while leveraging a provident fund and NPS for disciplined, long-term savings. Avoid retirement insurance schemes if the returns don't beat inflation—focus on term insurance instead.

In your 20s and 30s? Your best bet is to go heavier on equity and let compounding work its magic. In your 50s and 60s? Consider shifting to safer debt-based options to preserve your wealth.

There's no single way to save for retirement. It needs to be approached from multiple perspectives—and multiple financial instruments. Whether you want to move back to your home town in the interior corners of your state, or put your feet up in a coastal city abroad, or travel for 9 months of the year, or just spend your time chasing your grandkids, your corpus—and your retirement plans—solidify only when you have 2-3 investments working to achieve them.

What Does Retirement Look Like?—The TL; DR

Not Flower, FIRE

The FIRE movement, which encourages aggressive saving and frugality to retire early, is fast gaining popularity among millennial and Gen-Z professionals. But while it sounds amazing in theory, it often means sacrificing lifestyle joys like travel and socialising for decades.

How Much Money Do You Actually Need?

A common benchmark: Save 30 times your annual expenses.

For example, if you spend ₹12 lakh a year, you'd need

₹3.6 crores to retire comfortably. But the real number depends on your retirement vision—whether you're planning to move abroad, support family, or live simply.

The Inflation Factor

Inflation erodes your savings. What costs ₹1,000 today might cost ₹2,000 or more in 20 years. Retirement plans need to account for both pre- and post-retirement inflation.

Grow a Tree or Finish the Basket?

- ⇨ **Tree Approach:** Build a large sum (like a family inheritance) that generates income indefinitely.
- ⇨ **Basket Approach:** Accumulate a corpus to withdraw from gradually, even if it eventually runs out.

PF and NPS

- ⇨ **Provident Fund (PF):** Mandatory for most salaried employees, it's a tax-efficient, fixed-interest savings option. Contributions earn interest and can only be withdrawn fully after 58 years of age (with exceptions for emergencies).
- ⇨ **NPS:** Offers higher potential returns through investments in equity, bonds, and government securities. However, it mandates that 40% of the total corpus be used to buy an annuity, which provides a monthly pension.

Beware of Retirement Plans from Insurance Companies

Retirement annuity plans often promise 'guaranteed returns' but typically offer just 4-6% annual returns—barely keeping up with inflation. Separate insurance from investment: Buy term insurance for life cover and use mutual funds, provident fund, or NPS for growth.

The Ideal Retirement Portfolio

A balanced portfolio includes mutual funds for growth and safe options like PF and NPS for stability. Younger professionals can go heavy on equity for long-term gains, while those nearing retirement should shift toward safer debt-based options.

Notes

1. Nandini Singh, 'India Among Top Overworked Nations, 51% employees Work 49+ Hours A Week', *Business Standard*, 20 September 2024. https://www.business-standard.com/india-news/india-among-top-overworked-nations-51-employees-work-49-hours-a-week-124092000495_1.html
2. 'India Tops In Burnout Survey With 59% Reporting Symptoms', *Livemint,* 3 November 2023. https://www.livemint.com/news/india/india-tops-in-workplace-burnout-survey-with-59-reporting-symptoms-mckinsey-health-institute-11698999238983.html
3. Prime Investor Retirement Calculator: https://primeinvestor.in/calculators/retirement-calculator/Clear Tax Retirement Calculator: https://cleartax.in/s/retirement-planning-calculator

Epilogue

I feel a bit out of breath right now, to be honest. If you've come this far and feel the same way, know that it's normal. Also bask in the knowledge that you now know more about personal finance than you did before. That you can now make informed decisions about your finances.

That you can speak the language of money.

But just like any language, finance is dynamic. And the only way to improve your language and become a native speaker is to read more and speak more. Talk to your friends, your family, your colleagues, and your helpers about finance. Speak freely, speak often. You'll be a master in no time.

Here's wishing you prosperity.

Acknowledgements

Writing this book has made me a firm believer in the adage that things will take their own time, and that the best laid plans can be put to rest. From the first proposal I wrote in 2018 to the final manuscript that's in your hands today, it's been a ride.

I'm deeply grateful to my wonderful editor at Simon and Schuster India, Megha Mukherjee, whose not-so-gentle prodding is the reason the book is in your hands today. To Shephali, Vivek, Sarthak, and Aditi—you agreed to be a part of this book with zero notice and maximum grace, and I'm forever grateful.

Writing a book is hard enough, but writing it while working a full-time role? Slightly unhinged. It would've been easy to give the project up altogether, but I didn't, because of my immensely supportive workplace at ACKO—thank you for always encouraging me to be my best self.

And finally, no book is possible without the love, support and validation that cranky writers crave.

To Suhrith, my husband-slash-proofreader-slash-cheerleader-slash-therapist: Thank you for letting me yell, 'Can you read this once?' at you 432 times and never once flinching when I asked, 'But is it *really* good-good or are you just saying that?'

And last, but never least, to my beautiful family—this is for you, this is because of you.

About the Author

Lavanya Mohan is a CA turned writer from Chennai. She leads the charter for content and social media marketing at one of India's most prominent insurtech companies. Her words have been published in *The Hindu*, *BuzzFeed India*, *Vogue Business*, *ELLE India* and *FirstPost*. A self-confessed money nerd, she has written extensively about personal finance through her columns, 'Bookkeeping' for *The Morning Context* and 'Rupee Rani' for *The News Minute*.

She writes about money on her blog, PennMoney (www.pennmoney.com) and can be found talking about it on Instagram, X and Substack as @lavsmohan.